MW01520110

"It has been such a deep hon
up to skillfully support others
mility, generosity, wisdom, an _____ _____ __ _____,
kindness, and intelligence and expertly supports couples in reconnecting
to the heart of what matters most in their relationships. His own em-
bodiment of what he teaches radiates from him and brings out the best
in those around him, inspiring individuals and couples alike. He has my
wholehearted recommendation!"

—Christine Eartheart

"It has been a true pleasure working with Jack. His genuine and compassionate nature coupled with years of experience sets Jack apart as an in-
valuable resource that has proven to be a beacon of insight and wisdom.
Practical tools and exercises provided by Jack are exceptionally effective
in promoting self-awareness and understanding within the dynamics of
relationships. Whether it's communication strategies, conflict resolution
techniques, or fostering intimacy, Jack equips ministry leaders with tangible skills that can be immediately applied to their most important
relationship."

—Rick and Lynn Jenkins

"If you are like eighty percent of ministry leaders who feel their marriage
has been negatively impacted by their ministry, then I highly recommend you check out 1 Heart Coaching. Dr. Jack Taylor has both the
training and commitment to help your marriage go to the next levels of
health and intimacy."

—Steve Sundby, Founder, Two Step Coaching + Consulting

"Dr. Jack Taylor is a ministry veteran who has given his life to helping
others, including those leading churches and on the fringes of society.
Through years of service, he has maintained both wisdom and

compassion, placing people before the systems and business of ministry. Speaking out of his concern for others and ability to build quality one-to-one relationships, Jack will be able to speak into your marriage with a wealth of experience and expertise."

—Dr. David Horita, Regional Director, Fellowship Pacific

"In the tumultuous times we are in, leaders need to take a step back and ensure not only their own emotional and spiritual health, but prioritize the health of their marriage and family. Jack and Gayle have been through the vicissitudes of ministry life and know what takes to go the distance. My wife and I can speak from experience: You will only be enriched by time spent with them!"

—Pastor Jeremy MacDonald, Lead Pastor,
Faith Fellowship Baptist Church

"Jack and Gayle and my wife and I have journeyed beside each other for over forty years, both in Kenya and Vancouver. I can attest to the pressures and pains this couple have faced and the support they have offered countless others from over fifty ethnic backgrounds. Needless to say, they have enormous hearts of compassion and incredible wisdom to offer others. In the pressure cooker of life, they have also prioritized their marriage and family relationships with a view to health and growth, whatever the cost.

"Today's leaders, both new and seasoned, face incredibly unique challenges. The failures of current and former leaders are emblazoned across the internet. The expectations of followers are very different. Respect must be earned, not assumed. Societal pressures on their own marriages and families continue to grow exponentially. Seasoned leaders cannot afford to coast on past experience for relational health. They must be lifelong learners committed to growth. This is where the partnership with an experienced coach is priceless."

—Pastor Mark Buhler, Missionary, Fellowship International

"I would wholeheartedly recommend 1 Heart Coaching as it enables couples to flourish in their marriages and impact their spheres of influence. For almost a decade, I have enjoyed the privilege of meeting in an accountability/friendship trio with Jack Taylor. Jack and his wife Gayle shine with an authenticity that overflows into wise counsel and humble, effective leadership. Time spent with this couple will be a strategic investment in your marriage and leadership capacity.

"Leaders today live in a cultural fishbowl. They can no longer pretend that their personal lives do not spill into their public personas. I highly recommend 1 Heart as a resource that will share the tools of a dynamic, healthy marriage so that leaders can cause their spouses to flourish and their spheres of influence to thrive."

—Pastor David MacBain, Fellowship Pastor

JACK A. TAYLOR

WHEN *Ministry*
AND
Marriage
COLLIDE

Honest Conversations on Thriving through Conflict

Printed in Canada

ISBN: 978-1-4866-2567-3
eBook ISBN: 978-1-4866-2565-9

Word Alive Press
119 De Baets Street Winnipeg, MB R2J 3R9
www.wordalivepress.ca

WORD ALIVE
—P R E S S—

MIX
Paper | Supporting
responsible forestry
FSC   FSC® C103567
www.fsc.org

Cataloguing in Publication information can be obtained from Library and Archives Canada.

This book is dedicated with thanks to Bret and Christine Eartheart for their work with Thriving Relationship Coaches everywhere; to Gayle as the heart of my heart for forty-seven years; and to all seasoned leaders who are stretching themselves to strengthen their great covenant as they fulfill their Great Commission in line with the great commandment.

CONTENTS

ACKNOWLEDGEMENTS   xi

INTRODUCTION   xiii
    Leadership Couples   xvi
    The Five Stages of Thriving Relationships   xxi

QUAGMIRE ONE
Identity

Identity and Individuality: Who are you?   2
Identity and Ministry   7
Identity and Intersectionality   11
Identity and Vision   16
Identity and Personalities   20
Identity and Friendship   26
Identity and Responsibility   30

QUAGMIRE TWO
Attachment

Attachment and Relationship   38
Attachment and Feelings   44
Attachment and Cycles   51
Attachment and Raw Spots   57
Attachment and Forgiveness   61
Attachment and Stories   66
Attachment and Panic   70

QUAGMIRE THREE
Calling

Calling: Why Do You Do What You Do?   77
Calling as a Target   78
Calling and Theology   81

Calling and Convictions   85
Calling and Strengths   90
Calling and Schedule   94
Calling and Communication   101
Calling and Authority   104

QUAGMIRE FOUR
Family

Family and Parenting   109
Family and Rules   113
Family and In-Laws   118
Family and Finances   121
Family and Roles   126
Family and Infidelity   131
Family and Culture   137

QUAGMIRE FIVE
Intimacy

Intimacy and Busyness   144
Intimacy and the Love Account   148
Intimacy and Connection Rituals   152
Intimacy and Emotional Connections   157
Intimacy and Fears   161
Intimacy and Heart Listening   165
Intimacy: Brakes and Accelerators   170
Intimacy and Abuse   175

CONCLUSION   183

APPENDIX: PERSONALITY   195

ENDNOTES   203

BIBLIOGRAPHY   209

ABOUT THE AUTHOR   211

ACKNOWLEDGEMENTS

To my partner in life, love, and faith: Gayle; to my children and their spouses: Richard and Ericka, Michelle and Tyler, Laura and Marc, Tam and Graham; and to my incredible grandchildren, who have lived out love. To my mentors, Christine and Bret, at Thriving Relationship Coaching, who have provided many of the practical tools I have included in this work. And to my clients and colleagues who have shared so many conversations with me through the years.

INTRODUCTION

This is an exciting time for seasoned ministry leaders to model lasting love in a society so quick to discard it. While we live in an age where convenience and connection make lasting love easier, we also live in a world where distractions and disconnections make lasting love more challenging.

There are numerous high-quality books on marriage available already. There are more on leadership. Perhaps a good number on conflict management. *When Ministry and Marriage Collide* is an offering from an insider's perspective. I've been married forty-seven years, been in leadership for forty-three, been a counselor for over thirty, and now work as a certified relationship coach. I've worked internationally in missions for eighteen years, pastored a multicultural faith community for twenty-three, helped launch nine nonprofit ministries, and sat or advised on numerous boards.

This book is also a recognition of a reality that Scripture acknowledges:

> An unmarried man is concerned about the Lord's affairs—how he can please the Lord. But a married man is concerned about the affairs of this world—how he can please his wife— and his interests are divided. An

unmarried woman or virgin is concerned about the Lord's affairs: her aim is to be devoted to the Lord in both body and spirit. But a married woman is concerned about the affairs of this world—how she can please her husband. (1 Corinthians 7:32-34)

Resilient relationship is crucial for seasoned leaders. We read enough biographies and testimonials of those who have burned out or lost their relationship through poor choices and relationship breakdown. Many times, the marriage relationship breakdowns seem to come from an inability to resolve conflict. We are uncomfortable with the options that face us: to speak truth in love, hoping for a resilient and dynamic partnership, or to stay numb and dumb, fearing rejection and abandonment that could leave us alone.

By God's grace, we have been given a partner who is designed to stand with us as we face our fiercest dragons, soar to our highest heights, and walk through the deepest shadows of our inner selves. No one else will know the best and worst of us like this one will. They will woo out the divine image, sift the chaff from the wheat, nurture the light during dark times, and call us to the freedom we were designed for. And as they do for us, so we will do for them—if we understand how.

Our marital relationship anchors all we do. When we feel deeply connected with our partner, we are more effective in our work and contented in our other relationships. Coaching helps bring about alignment in communication, conflict resolution, and satisfaction in our intimacy.

As those made in God's image, we are designed for social connection. The fear of disconnection strikes to the core of our being, and yet, in the midst of an emotional storm, we so often fail to reconnect. Thriving marital relationships are forged through a five-level process with proven tools to manage the journey.

When Ministry and Marriage Collide focuses on seven couples talking through five marriage quagmires with their coach: Identity, Attachment, Calling, Family, and Intimacy. While it's not exactly a workbook, there are tools laid out that can be utilized to help you walk through whatever you are facing in these areas. This book is not designed to solve all your conflicts, but to help you recognize the diversity of conflicts impacting ministry and marriage as well as the diversity of help available. My goal is to encourage you to utilize that help and to see that conflict is a path toward growth.

A successful marriage requires falling in love many times, always with the same person.[1]

The challenge of this quote from Mignon McLaughlin is that our partner is always changing—and so are we. With everything else in life changing as well, it is easy to get stuck along the way.

How does a leadership couple recognize that their ministry and marriage may be stuck in a quagmire? That despite the external praise of others, their internal dreams and goals may be crashing? What is a quagmire when it comes to relationship? And if you get stuck in one, how do you get out? We're here to explore all of this through honest conversations.

This book is designed as a companion volume to use with a relationship coach but can be used separately if you so desire. Take your time and apply what you can.

Most Christian weddings will include a reading from 1 Corinthians 13:4-8, which says:

> Love is patient, love is kind. It does not envy, it does
> not boast, it is not proud. It does not dishonor others,
> it is not self-seeking, it is not easily angered, it keeps
> no record of wrongs. Love does not delight in evil but
> rejoices with the truth. It always protects, always trusts,
> always hopes, always perseveres. Love never fails.

If we applied this to our everyday marriage covenant relationship, there would be little conflict to speak of. There is something wired deep within that tests the limits of each of these characteristics of love. Seasoned leaders are not free of this inner reality—especially when they are stretched by numerous demands and expectations.

Now imagine, if you will, a low-rise commercial building. The elevator opens to a sign leading you to the reception area of a corner office. Outside the office door sits an olive wood coat hanger, and once inside, you notice a Persian carpet welcoming you to stand and look through the floor-to-ceiling windows at the city below. To your right, there's a laptop opened on a mahogany desk, with a plushy loveseat in front of it, and two padded office chairs to the side. There's a counter with coffee and tea set up, and a water cooler perched beside it. A bookshelf, stuffed with various books, sits against the wall, and behind the desk are artifacts from Africa, India, China, and the Middle East inset here and there.

This is the setting where significant conversations are about to happen.

LEADERSHIP COUPLES

Let's meet the couples who will share their conversations.

Jim and Sharon realized they were in a quagmire when their heated discussion uncovered a complicated situation they didn't know how to escape. They had navigated skillfully through their first- and seventh-year marital challenges, and after celebrating a decade in ministry, had settled into a routine of how to manage life. What appeared to be a scheduling conflict around where holidays would be spent turned into a rapidly sinking swampland about control, manipulation, emotions, and unfaithfulness.

What kind of an honest conversation would you have with Jim and Sharon? Relationship quagmires may involve strong emotions where former best friends dance through their fear, guilt, and shame with fight, flight, freeze, or fawning responses. Routines may camouflage unresolved issues, and being nice is not always the best way to escape the unseen minefields and hot spots that arise when marriage and ministry collide.

Sam and Hannah rocked their friends when, after spending a week at a women's retreat, Hannah emailed Sam that she would be taking an extended time away. Sam's role as a prominent seminarian absorbed much of his energy, and the unexpected task of being the primary caregiver for his three children left him panicking and drawing on others to talk sense into his wife. When Hannah's social media accounts boasted pictures of her in a new job and a new apartment, Sam came unglued.

What kind of an honest conversation would you have with Sam and Hannah? It is not surprising that lack of good communication is at the heart of many quagmires. The model of our family of origin and the way we've learned to attach to our partner to get our needs met both have a strong impact on how we bond. Our understanding of our own feelings, as well as how we express them, can also impact the effectiveness of our communication.

Francis and Nyota had drifted apart after a dozen years in the busyness of ministry. Work demands, technology pulls, and the unceasing expectations of needy community members were a constant reality. The two of them had also aligned themselves with different social causes that continued to sap up their focus. It was at a convention that Francis cringed under the convicting message about date nights, regular intimacy, and shared spiritual disciplines. His enthusiastic return to an empty home left him confused and wondering what to do next. In this case, Nyota had raced to spend a weekend with a friend in need, but the shock of what could have been stimulated them to rethink the current status of their marriage.

What kind of honest conversation would you have with Francis and Nyota? Rarely do newlyweds plan to drift apart, but the best of us can get waylaid by busyness and demands. The expectations of others can stretch us further than we can give. These are human quagmires frequently encountered by leaders. They are difficult and sticky situations that aren't easy to escape without assistance. There are no simple solutions. What have others done?

Gerhard and Isabella were veteran missionaries with seventeen years of translation experience. Gerhard completed seminary in Germany and joined a translation team in Congo where Isabella had come from Brazil to work as a nurse. An auto accident in his early years left Gerhard with a limp, and without parents. His uncle, a minister, raised him with a firm hand and a distant heart. His aunt was distracted with four other children whom she homeschooled. Isabella's mother died of a fever when Isabella was ten, so she stepped in as mother to her three younger siblings while trying to complete her own education. Her career, her mission work, and her marriage all seemed like an escape from home until they started feeling like their own form of trap. It was clear her husband didn't value her culture, thoughts, or family as much as she did. She searched online for a relationship coach.

What kind of honest conversation would you have with Gerhard and Isabella? Although it's a cliché that we should look back to move forward, it is an important part of growth to realize the impact that our family of origin has had on how we currently relate. The models we've observed and the experiences we have endured affect us deeply. In our marriage relationships, we're often trying to duplicate what we knew— or we are reacting against it.

Hailey and Simon launched a counseling ministry focused on at-risk youth. Their clients were heavy on demand and low on resources, but the two of them found ways to accommodate for their schedule and activities. With their phones constantly ringing, meals together became few and far between. Eight years into their sacrificial work, several of their clients had become dependent enough to feel more like family. Boundaries were blurred and resentments continued to surface— frequently over a lack of energy for intimate time together. When a holiday got cancelled to deal with an emergency, Simon's father suggested that the couple might need outside help.

What kind of honest conversation would you have with Hailey and Sam? Most quagmires begin innocently enough with a sincere desire to make a difference. Leaders are often wired to serve others, and there is a sense of value in pouring into the life of another person. Things like margin, time together, and healthy boundaries with dependent clients can be compromised, ultimately impacting the marital relationship. Resentment grows slowly when someone outside the relationship draws increasingly more time and energy. Refocusing priorities and setting clear boundaries is essential.

Ben and Susan felt a common conviction to leave their chosen careers and join in ministry with a congregation. Both had attended three years of seminary before their first child was born. They had loved to lead worship together, but Susan paused this to focus on raising their son and doing her courses online. Meanwhile, Ben saturated his mind with doctoral studies and church planting. While a small group of eager learners met for a year in their home, it was easy to share their gifts with satisfaction. When an amenities room opened up in a community hall—and a second child arrived—Ben took on the primary oversight of the growing group and found others to provide hospitality and encouragement for new arrivals. Five years into the church plant, Susan found herself stuck in a makeshift nursery, looking after the little ones whose parents gurgled their praise about Ben. One Sunday, she stepped out of the swarm of writhing little bodies and glanced into the sanctuary, where she was gobsmacked to witness the adoring gaze exchanged by her husband and the female worship leader as they shared a duet. An emptiness swept over her, and during a walk that afternoon, she poured out her sense of abandonment to her husband.

What kind of honest conversation would you have with Ben and Susan? Abandonment arises in so many ways among leadership marriages. It may not be a sexual affair, but the internal feelings of betrayal have all the hallmarks of it. A mistress can take many forms: work, technology, hobbies, and addictions are just a few examples. To make light of a partner's sense of distancing, even if no physical affair is happening, only accentuates the depth of the quagmire.

Esther and Phil had developed a progressive relationship. Esther accepted an executive role in her congregation as a leader of ministries, and Phil built an online business at home while managing the household. Each week they set up their calendar appointments to avoid unnecessary conflicts, but as time passed, it seemed that the ministries were demanding more and more time with the never-ending staffing issues, events, and organizational meetings. For ten years Phil said nothing, but inside, he sensed a lonely restlessness he couldn't fathom. There seemed to be no room for his input on decisions when it came to events, finances, or social outings. Something deep and dark was swallowing his sense of who he was, and a strong guilt grew as his time on the computer took him to places he had never thought possible. When Esther impulsively opened his laptop to access a small group study, she was shocked at what she found.

What kind of honest conversation would you have with Esther and Phil? The sense of identity and calling can strain the ties that bind when spouses' paths diverge. The sense of togetherness dissipates, and two lonely pilgrims try to make sense of where the road divided. When we start to feel our partner doesn't value us because they have no time for us, we can enter a quagmire that may get us in over our head.

At times it may seem that the one who pledged their love and life to us has forgotten every part of our vows. A foundational thing to believe is that conflict is growth waiting to happen. Another thing to remember is that, if you are a person of faith, that your prayer and spiritual disciplines together are more than rituals. Wise friends, a counselor, and accountability partners are more than busy spaces on your calendar.

Before we look at specific quagmires, it is important to realize the stages that thriving relationships grow through. As you read through these stages, see if you can identify which stage you and your partner might be in.

THE FIVE STAGES OF THRIVING RELATIONSHIPS

Romance: Most relationships— that aren't arranged in advance—start with some form of attraction, bonding, hopefulness, perhaps ecstasy, and bliss. You may have acted out your best behavior, focused on the best of your partner, given freely without scorekeeping, and felt that surge of passion and vitality.

Power Struggle: Inevitably, once the newness and vitality of the relationship starts to grow into a rhythm, other realities arise. For some reason, you may react negatively and habitually with your partner. You may feel disillusioned, angry, annoyed, disappointed, confused, or frustrated. You might notice conflict, secrets that surface, disconnection, settling, lack of desire—even blame and criticism. When you examine your partnership, it may suddenly feel uninspiring and stuck in a repetitive cycle, with less intimacy and emotional attachment. This is normal to experience, but it's not where you want to remain.

Commitment: Eventually, and perhaps with outside assistance, there needs to be movement toward the stage that follows the power struggle. Both partners need to powerfully commit to whatever is necessary for moving the relationship toward thriving and the best version of yourselves. Two questions need to be explored at this stage: "What does this relationship need from me to thrive?" and "How have I been contributing to what hasn't been working – and how do I need to change and grow?" This stage is not the end, however.

Growth: If the relationship is to thrive, there needs to be a threefold understanding. Partner one must be committed to external and internal growth; partner two must be committed to external and internal growth; and both partners must be committed to the relationship's growth together. This involves an increasing awareness of what's been going on underneath the challenges you've been facing. It means learning to break through issues that have gridlocked the relationship. It requires applying new tools regularly, becoming more intentional, experiencing greater ease with each other, gaining more understanding, deeper connection, renewed hope, and finding joy in the journey.

Thriving: This is where we want all our marriages to be. Here's where we are sharing an inspiring vision together that draws us forward into our future. We experience full safety and trust with each other in all areas of life. We develop a spirit of teamwork, togetherness, aliveness. We work to make our dreams come true. Our communication is healthy, positive, and open, and we feel seen and valued. We experience and express daily appreciation, respond to challenges with shared wisdom, and sense true fulfillment. Passion and romance are strong. Connection, secure attachment, and true love are firmly in place.

Alert: No relationship flows smoothly through these five stages. Collapsing back into the power struggle will happen over and over. By recognizing this reality and embracing the resiliency and strength of your relationship, your stays there will be shorter, and your recommitments sweeter. Many of the quagmires I present in this book show up in the second stage, during power struggles.[2]

QUAGMIRE ONE

Identity

**"The things that make me different
are the things that make me."**
—Piglet

The issue of identity has risen to the forefront for leaders as they navigate the complexities of ministry and marriage. Through the global exposure of technology, it is easy to feel the pressure of comparing yourself to others, of functioning out of fear, and of measuring your value by what others think—or what you think they think. It is tempting to move from one opportunity to the next to discover meaning and satisfaction. And it's tempting to be someone in the limelight that you aren't at home, where the masks can come off, and where insecurities can find shadowy expression.

Several factors come into play when ministry and marriage collide over identity. These may include the factors that make us individuals (birth order, ethnicity, etc.) or the influence of current social thinking (like intersectionality). Who we think we are in ministry and marriage can also be influenced by our visions, our personality, our friendships, and our roles or responsibilities.

Marriage is so much more than understanding who I am. It is understanding who we are.

Too often, we look in the mirror and all we see is me.

IDENTITY AND INDIVIDUALITY: WHO ARE YOU?

Jim and Sharon finished their paperwork with the receptionist and stood shoulder-to-shoulder in my office pointing out sights on the skyline. As I set up the space, Jim nodded and handed over the sheet of goals for our time together. They slumped into the loveseat and shifted until they felt comfortable. After a brief interaction, we started an honest conversation about facing this quagmire of identity.

"I don't know who I am anymore," Sharon said. "It all seemed fine when we started our relationship. I knew Jim was called into the ministry, and I went along for the ride. I said the vows about his people being my people, and his God being my God, but I didn't realize that I was going to lose who I was." She shifted in her chair, glancing at Jim for reassurance. "The first year was kind of an adjustment hell, but we made it. We changed jobs in the seventh year and went through a time where I thought we were going to break. Over and over, I am the one who has to let go of my relationships and start all over again."

Jim reached over and gave Sharon's hand a squeeze. "We were both raised with the traditional view that the man is the leader who gets the call, and the woman looks after the home. Sharon had so many gifts that the people in our community elevated her to positions of responsibility, but things got tense when it was hard to be fully present for the kids and the community as well. I think the people in our first community missed her more than they missed me. They keep calling her and expecting her to have time for them like before."

I couldn't help smiling. "The question of identity has raged to the fore in our day. How do you define yourself? By what priority do you determine identity: by faith, nationality, birthplace, cultural ethnicity, education, employment position, birth family, marital status, birth order, personality, gender, family role, strengths? Have you had time to consider all this?"

Sharon jumped in. "I've probably thought about a few of those things, but not really had time to consider how it affects our relationship. We're both believers, of course, I'm a firstborn, and Jim is an only child. His family is richer than mine, but we've done okay."

"Do you know Anthony Kiedis?" I asked.

"You mean the guy with the Red Hot Chili Peppers?" Jim responded. "No, his uncle. Same name. He says that 'until you settle your identity, you will live in leadership insecurity.'³ Insecurity is a sure recipe for collision in marriage and ministry."

"You can say that again," Sharon said. "I thought I was the one with a lost identity—and insecurity—until we had that big fight. Jim unloaded on me about being controlling and emotional, and I accused him of being manipulative and unfaithful."

"How did it all start?" I asked.

Jim shifted in his chair and raised his hand. "It was me. We usually schedule things a month in advance, and I got busy and didn't take the time to let her know that the board chair had scheduled a vision retreat on the weekend after Thanksgiving. Sharon knows that is always a time when we visit her folks, so she had booked the tickets without talking to me."

"Ooops!" I said. "Definitely sounds like a collision. There's a leadership guru named Crawford Loritts Jr. who says, 'never underestimate the power of self-deception and the pull toward self-reliance.'⁴ He sees the primary identity of ministry leaders as formed through suffering, struggle, failure, and hard-fought successes.⁵ Seems like you've faced some of that."

"We could use some of those successes," Jim said. "It seems that since the impact of Covid on our church and society, we've been languishing and trying to survive our ministry and our marriage."

"Languishing is a real thing," I said, "but could your current marriage challenges be part of the refining process of who you are becoming? Out of the eight billion humans on this planet, there are no other two like you and your spouse. The question of identity is a clarifying one when it comes to ministry."

Jim rose and took time to fill his glass at the water cooler. "I'm still not sure why identity is so important to Sharon. When we got married, we made a covenant to be one. Why is this so important?"

"What was the question Jesus asked his followers in Caesarea Philippi?" I asked.

"Who do people say I am?" Jim answered.

"And what was the next question?"

Sharon leaned forward. "*But who do you say I am?*" (Matthew 16:15)

"That's the question of identity. Jesus had already been affirmed at his baptism when his Father announced his identity, and that laid the foundation of assurance for all that would follow.[6] When we work with each other, it's important that we know who we are—but also that those we work with know who we are as well. That's true for husbands and wives, and for congregants."

"So, you're saying that we act out of who we think we are," Sharon said. "That this question of identity hits at the core of our being when we make decisions in our ministry or marriage."

"Yes!" I picked up a handout and found the quote I was looking for. "Bill Howatt, Founder and CEO of Howatt HR says:"

> The mark of a good leader is defined by how you show up each day, respond to stressful challenges and behave in good and challenging times. … As a leader, you're defined by every interaction related to your readiness to lead and deal with challenges and opportunities as they occur. Understanding your leadership identity begins with how you view yourself and how you show up to work each day regarding your attitude, mindset and mental and physical energy.[7]

"I can see how that applies for work," Jim said, "but we're dealing with our marriage."

"What is true for the identity and character of a leader in the workplace is also true in the home. Part of the collision for leaders comes when who they are at home is far different than who they are in public."

"What can we do about our relationship?" Sharon asked. "I always feel like I'm dealing with the trap of comparing myself with my husband, or half a dozen other successful women in our community. I'm always mindreading because he doesn't tell me anything anymore."

I passed her a handout with three interlocking circles. "Any formula for lasting relationship growth involves three factors. For both partners, there must be equal inner growth, which involves self-awareness, inner resourcing, cultivation of core beliefs, healing, and intentional commitment to the other. There must also be external growth, which embraces new actions and reactions to the circumstances you are in. Your growth and your partner's growth are both essential." She held it out for Jim to see better. "The third factor is the growth of your combined relationship through an intentional and deliberate effort to establish safe and secure attachment, plus the implementation of tools and strategies for healthy communication, support, and connection.[8] We're not working to compare our growth against each other's, but to team up so both of you are growing."

"I thought attachment had to do with children and parents," Sharon said.

"We'll talk more about this another time," I said, "but attachment theory believes that the safety and security we felt in our family of origin, or other past relationships, impacts how safe and secure we feel in our current relationship. It is about how we give and receive love."

Sharon released the handout and tapped on Jim's wrist. "Now, that explains a lot about why you have trouble feeling safe with me. It doesn't take much time with your mother before I understand you completely."

"It isn't that bad," Jim said.

I held up my hand. "One more thing before I give you another handout. As leaders, we can look at our identity in one of three ways. First, we can think that what we have determines what we do, and therefore who we are. Secondly, we can think that what we do determines what we have, and therefore who we are. Or finally, we can believe that who we are unleashes what we do and then what we have. Differing beliefs in this area will create its own conflicts. Aligning our goals, beliefs, and values at the core of who we are is essential."

Those three formulas look something like the diagram below. Where does your identity come from?

Have ⟶ Do ⟶ Be

Do ⟶ Have ⟶ Be

Be ⟶ Do ⟶ Have

"Maybe we need some time to think through all this," Jim said. "Our conflict might be rooted in some of what we've talked about today."

"Just so you are aware," I said, "sixty-nine percent of conflicts are considered perpetual. In other words, you may be dealing with the same thing over and over again.[9] The key to a solid marriage might be figuring out how to deal with those immoveable problems along the way. Having a sense of humor is helpful. When you married, you chose a group of unsolvable issues to wrestle with. What you don't want happening is emotional disengagement and broken trust that traps you in gridlock."

"How do we know if we're in gridlock?" Jim asked.

I rummaged through my binder and extracted a single sheet of paper. "Here are eight signs to cause concern:"

- The conflict makes you feel rejected by your partner.
- You keep talking about it but make no headway.
- You become entrenched in your positions and are unwilling to budge.
- When you discuss the subject, you end up feeling more frustrated and hurt.
- Your conversations about the problems are devoid of humor, amusement, or affection.
- You become even more 'unbudgeable' over time, which leads you to vilify each other during these conversations.
- This vilification makes you even more rooted in your positions—polarized, more extreme in your views, and less willing to compromise.
- Eventually you disengage from each other emotionally.[10]

"Even if you see these characteristics to some degree in your conflicts, there is still a way to escape gridlock if you're motivated enough."

"What about solvable problems?" Jim asked.

"Generally, these kinds of problems are less painful, gut-wrenching, or intense. But that doesn't mean they go away easily. You still need to face them head on. Your identity can play a huge role in determining whether your issues are perpetual or solvable. Take some time this week to see if you can differentiate which of your issues are solvable and perpetual."

IDENTITY AND MINISTRY

> **"A great marriage is not when the 'perfect couple' comes together. It is when an imperfect couple learns to enjoy their differences."** — Dave Meurer[11]

Sam and Hannah were in the same quagmire of identity but dealing with it from a different angle. It took months after Hannah's departure before she was ready for a conversation. We'd already been through the awkward phases of the discussion around the separation before we faced the reality of how their marriage and ministry had collided. The two of them sat six feet apart in separate chairs, facing the loveseat where I was perched.

"Of course I left him," Hannah said. "He never, ever took time to learn anything about who I am. I was just another one of his minions— there to do what he needed me to do." She snapped her fingers. "Hannah, I need you to do this. Hannah, I need you to do that."

I took a deep breath and started. "I think I see part of the issue for you. There are six possible ways in which ministry and marriage might collide when it comes to identity. Both partners have ministry identities and personal identities. Collision might come between ministry identities, between personal identities, or between ministry and personal identities. Aligning all six is an art if we are to move toward a thriving relationship."

"What do you mean by that?" Sam asked.

I sorted through the files sitting beside me on the loveseat and handed both of them a drawing.

"I hope you're going to make sense of all this," Hannah said.

"Just take a moment to look it over first."

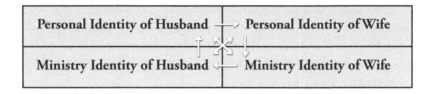

Personal Identity of Husband	→	Personal Identity of Wife
Ministry Identity of Husband	←	Ministry Identity of Wife

I tried to explain what they were looking at. "Identity is a complex and multidimensional reality which is constantly changing as we mature and encounter more and more of life. Who we are is influenced by individual experience, belief, growth, and personal alignment. Our faith, society, and culture help shape how we perceive ourselves and how we are perceived by others. Through our exploration, commitments, and consolidation, we develop character, strength, and direction. Our sense of belonging and acceptance within groups can motivate how we define and express our identity. Our sense of well-being and security can stimulate our mental health."

"Sounds complicated to me," Hannah said. "Why don't you say that when we don't see ourselves the way others see us that we'll end up fighting?"

Sam laid the paper down on his lap. "It could also be that we are pressured into being who we're not because we give in to what others expect us to be. I can see that my identity as a leader at church can't stay the same when I come home. I need to be a husband in my home, rather than a prof or a pastor."

Hannah sat up and turned toward him for the first time. "Wow! It took a special session to figure that out?" She folded up her paper. "And you need to realize that I am your wife—not one of your ministry leaders. I am not your slave, your volunteer, or your staff member."

I held up my hand again like a referee. "Internal conflicts around identity can arise when we try to reconcile who we believe we are with what society expects us to be. Or who our partner expects us to be. Stress and external messaging can cause us to repress aspects of who we think we are. Sometimes, ministry communities set up a triangle of leadership where the leader can be fast, cheap, or good—but can only be two of the three."

"What do you mean by that?" Sam asked.

I drew out a triangle with the three words at the points. "If you're good and fast you're likely not cheap. If you're fast and cheap you're likely not all that good. If you're cheap and good you're likely not all that fast. Of course, your leadership team or board still wants all three, and that can put pressure on you at work and at home."

Hannah nodded vigorously. "It's like when Sam tells me that suffering financially or staying overscheduled will only last for a season. They're sucking him dry, and I'm feeling it."

I tucked my handout back into the folder. "The respect and validation of others tend to draw out aspects of our identity that promote understanding and acceptance by others. If we have learned to be people pleasers, we may feel there is a whole layer of identity under the surface which we have never been free to explore or express."

"What about the traumas we have survived?" Hannah interrupted.

"Are you asking whether we label ourselves as a victim or an overcomer? As privileged or needy? As oppressed or oppressor?"

"Something like that," she said. "I've been through a lot even before meeting this guy. I have trouble with trust, and I'm in that space again."

"Maybe we should take a few minutes to look at rebuilding trust." I took out a handout and slid it across the desk. "Here are a few things for us to think through. You can keep the paper as a reminder."

Rebuilding trust. Ever had your trust violated? If you imagine trust as a tree, sometimes it seems you've had some significant branches hacked off. Sometimes it feels like the whole tree has been chopped down to the size of a stump. It takes time to rebuild trust, especially if there's been a radical violation of it. It can be done, however. Even a tree chopped down eventually puts out the smallest of shoots that arise from what was.

Rebuilding trust can be a challenging process, but it is possible with time, effort, and commitment. Here are ten ways to rebuild trust in a relationship, whether it's a personal or professional one:

1. **Apologize sincerely**: Acknowledge mistakes—or the breach of trust—then offer a heartfelt apology for the specific action or behavior. This is a good place to start.

2. **Take responsibility**: Accept complete responsibility for your actions and avoid making excuses or blaming others.

3. **Be transparent:** Practice honest communication by sharing your thoughts, feelings, and intentions with the other person in a transparent way.

4. **Listen actively**: Care about the other person's perspective and feelings by listening attentively without judgment.

5. **Make amends**: Take specific action, compromise, or pursue restitution that will rectify the situation.

6. **Set boundaries**: Clarify commitments and boundaries consistently to prevent future trust issues.

7. **Show consistency**: Demonstrate consistency in words and actions to show you can be relied on over time.

8. **Patience and understanding**: Recognize the other person's doubts and fears as you show patience and understanding.

9. **Seek professional help**: Access the guidance of a therapist, counselor, or coach to help rebuild trust.

10. **Keep promises**: Dedicate yourself to keeping commitments and promises as you embrace respect for the other person's feelings.

Remember that trust can be fragile, and it may take time to fully restore it. The process of rebuilding trust requires sincerity, effort, and a genuine desire to mend the relationship.

"You realize how hard this is for me, don't you?" Hannah said. "I may need a special session before we get too far."

"We'll definitely take time to process some of that," I said. "In the meantime, I want you to think back on your love story—on what brought you two together. What filled you with delight at that time, and what happened to the delight? When did things change? What stands in the way of that delight surfacing again?" I waited a moment as Hannah and Sam thought. "Lastly, I want you to focus on this from your side of things. Don't think about what has changed in your partner to steal your delight. Focus on yourself. What has changed in you that has robbed your delight, and what can you do to try and restore it again?"

"I thought we were looking forward," Hannah said.

"We are," I said. "Sometimes, there are things from the past anchoring us in place, and it is good to acknowledge those realities so we can let go of them and advance in our relationships. Sometimes it is also good practice to see what allowed us to move forward before this."

"But how do we manage our conflicts?" Hannah asked.

"There are a few keys to keep in mind," I said. "First, allow for negative emotions.[12] If your partner is angry, sad, disappointed, or afraid, that means it's time to stop and listen. You can understand a lot if you'll stop and listen to your partner. Second, this isn't about right and wrong. This is about relationship. Two people with their own thoughts, feelings, opinions, dreams, and desires are trying to forge a union of love. Third, accept your partner as someone on your team. You can't move forward unless you get to the point where your partner believes that you understand, accept, and maybe even respect them. Fourth, work for admiration. You may not be able to appreciate everything about your partner, but focus on something you can admire them for, and communicate that."

"Okay. Hopefully having this checklist will simplify a few things," Sam said.

IDENTITY AND INTERSECTIONALITY

"The secret of a happy marriage is finding the right person. You know they're right if you love to be with them all the time." — Julia Child[13]

Gerhard and Isabella took their time examining the curios as we prepared to meet. The clouds were dark and heavy this morning, and I hoped that had nothing to do with their gloomy facial expressions. It didn't take long to realize that this pair had the same issue of identity, just from another angle. They each came from different cultures (Germany and Brazil), had worked in a third culture (Congo), and were now living in yet another culture (North America). Gerhard had been studying intersectionality as a way to understand the conflict he was having with Isabella.

I tried to explain the issue to Isabella as we sat together. Gerhard had been frustrated by his attempts. I had prepared yet another handout, and I gave this to both of them.

"Intersectionality has become a driving ideology of our times. People have been divided into those who dominate and those who are dominated, as well as those who have privilege and those without. How you see yourself matters in how you interact with others."

"Every time I think about this idea, I think about all those whiners claiming to be hard done by," Isabella said. "This has got to be a first world problem. In Latin America and Africa, we don't have time to waste on thinking how oppressed we are. We are oppressed. It's just a fact."

"You're mostly right," I said. "Take a look at this chart. It divides people into two distinct groups. See if it helps explain the way society understands identity as it shows up in relationship. Those who are labeled as cisgender, male, white, European, heterosexual, wealthy, able-bodied, credentialed, young, attractive, upper middle class, English speaking, pale-skinned, Gentile, and fertile occupy the upper half of the privilege and domination scale. Those who are transgender, female, black, non-European, LGBTQ+, financially insecure, disabled, nonliterate, old, unattractive, working class, English as second language, dark-skinned, Jewish, and infertile have been relegated to the oppressed side of the scale. The more characteristics you have on the right side scale the worse off you are in our world. Or so the thinking goes."

"It says what I already know," Isabella said. "Gerhard is privileged, and I am not."

"Who came up with these categories?" Gerhard said. "It all seems artificial to me."

"What do you notice about the categories?"

Privileged / Dominator	Oppressed / Dominated
Cisgender	Transgender
Male	Female
White	Black
European background	Non-European
Heterosexual	LGBTQ+
Wealthy	Financially insecure
Able-bodied	Disabled
Credentialed	Non-literate
Young	Old
Attractive	Unattractive
Upper middle class	Working class
English speaker	English as second language
Pale-skinned	Dark-skinned
Gentile	Jewish
Fertile	Infertile

"Which labels would you apply to yourself?" I asked.

Isabella examined the paper, underlining a few with a yellow highlighter I'd given her. "Female, non-European, financially insecure—

definitely not old—working class, English as a second language, darker skinned… that's enough. I just think that Gerhard doesn't value my culture, my thoughts, my family. He doesn't appreciate what I had to go through growing up. I already know I'm oppressed. I just feel trapped by it all."

I moved my chair closer, still six feet apart from the two of them. "The more labels you apply to yourself, the more reactive or resigned you might become in response to who others have declared you to be. You can see that the scale already presupposes how things work in a marriage relationship. You can also see that this is a first world-order stereotyping based on broad categorizations. Nevertheless, it might be good to see if this type of thinking has infiltrated any sense of who you think you are, or who you think your partner is. Love without labels is harder than it sounds."

"You can say that again," Gerhard said. "Funny thing is, I don't feel privileged, and I don't appreciate others thinking I am. I've given up everything for God—and for Isabella. I know what it is to be abandoned, to suffer, and to feel like a victim. I just don't think it helps to think about it."

"It only helps you to have a mirror into your own heart and into Isabella's heart," I said. "Sometimes we need a mirror because we don't understand how the thinking of the world around us is impacting us and our relationship. If there's a conflict going on it might be a good idea to see what truths, or lies, we're telling ourselves."

"Isn't there a verse about there not being any differences that matter?" Isabella asked.

I reached for my Bible and turned to Galatians 3:28. "You're probably thinking of this one," I said. *"There is neither Jew nor Gentile, neither slave nor free, nor is there male and female, for you are all one in Christ Jesus."*

"That's the one," Isabella said. "Things would be much better if we didn't set up artificial barriers because of how different we are. We start from what we have in common and then appreciate the differences from there."

"That sounds like a good idea," I said, "but there are a lot of ways in which seeing our differences helps bring understanding, empathy, and appreciation. Think of all the diversities of food out there. It's amazing how many ways you can prepare chicken or rice or vegetables. Every culture brings their own version for the benefit of us all. Why don't we take a moment to brainstorm what makes us unique as people? Isabella, you can start. Think of five things."

Isabella bit her lip for a moment. "We have different talents, personalities, beliefs, values, and traditions."

Gerhard accepted my nod. "We have different customs, art styles, sports, education, and levels of expertise."

"Does that mean we're oppressed if we don't have what others have? Anything else?"

"We have different careers, perspectives, fashions, hobbies, and pursuits," Isabella said.

Gerhard patted his wife's shoulder with a smile. "Those are good. How about different communication styles, genetic traits, accents, morals, and rituals?"

"I think we're seeing that there are thousands of ways to differentiate who we are from others, and that allowing ourselves to live within the reality of who we are—and accepting the reality of who our partner is—can help us love without labels." I stood up and walked around to the large round Persian carpet behind the love seat. "Stand up with me and look at this carpet. Which strand is the most important one to identify here?"

Gerhard knelt on it and ran his hand over it. "I imagine every strand is important."

"Yes, every strand of you is important for making you who you are. This is important to realize for yourself, but also for the one you love. Every strand is part of what makes you who you are."

"So I'm not a victim?" Isabella asked.

"Do you want to be?"

"Not really," she replied.

"Then, starting today, embrace who you are, and decide on how you're going to grow you from here."

IDENTITY AND VISION

"It makes such a difference to have someone who believes in you." —Winnie the Pooh

Esther and Phil arrived for their appointment, and it was immediately clear who was in charge. Esther marched in and pointed at the left side of the loveseat for Phil. He glanced my way and then slumped into his place. Esther draped her coat over the back of the loveseat, sat down on her side, and crossed her arms and legs.

"I've got another appointment in an hour, so thanks for meeting with us," Esther said. "Someone suggested we should see you, but I'm not sure yet what good it will do."

"Welcome," I said. "Do you have a vision for who you are, and how that impacts the vision for your relationship?"

"Not sure what vision there is at this point," she said. "I'm an executive leader who is busy, and Phil is a pornography addict who sits at home on his computer all day."

Phil crossed his arms and focused on his shoes. He said nothing.

"Do I see that you're resigned to living with that label?" I asked Phil.

He glanced up briefly and focused down again. "Of course, I don't like the label. Stuff happens. I just got tired of being at home day after day while Esther is off making a name for herself. She never has time for me. I never dreamed I'd fall for this stuff."

"So, let's imagine that you two actually had time for each other," I said. "What character-building activities would you want to fill your time with when you are together? Let's focus on using positive language."

"What's the point to this?" Esther asked. "He's the one with the problem."

I leaned toward her. "It seems that your relationship is dictated by labels that you've attached to your individuality, and it seems that those labels are giving you a reason to not build a relationship together. I'm just wondering what kind of relationship you would want if there were no labels. What would your relationship be built on?"

"Trust, for sure," Esther said. "And faithfulness and real communication."

"Quality time together," Phil added. "And encouragement and affirmation."

"Okay. How do you want to communicate?"

"I'm fine with texts now and then," Esther said. "I'm definitely putting a filter on his laptop that alerts me to what he is watching."

"I'd love a note on the bathroom counter in the morning," Phil said. "Just letting me know when she'll be home and what she's doing all day. I'd be happy if she gave me a call at lunch, or even emailed me a short note saying she was thinking of me."

"How do you want to respond to conflict?"

Esther raised her hand. "I think Phil ought to see a counselor who can help him sort out his addiction issues. If he straightened that out, it would make all the difference."

"That may be true," I said. "But right now, we're focusing on how to grow the relationship the two of you will build. You need to be able to invest your whole selves into this."

"We have friends who we can talk with," Phil said.

Esther turned toward her husband with her fist propping up her jaw. "Who are you talking about? I don't want anyone in the church to know what you're doing."

"Maybe you two can work that out on a walk sometime," I said. "How do you want to support and love each other?"

"I think we need to schedule date nights again," Phil said. "It seems the needs of Esther's work trump any of our time together, even if it's on the calendar."

"Fair enough," I said. "How do you want to, individually, manage stress and practice self-care?"

"I practice atomic habits," Esther said. "Every day I have my list, and I follow it. The only stress in my life, apart from work issues, is what this husband of mine is doing on his computer when I'm not around."

"I need to work on this," Phil said. "I tend to get stuck surfing the net, binging on shows, blogging, and emailing clients. A lot of screen time. I need to go for a walk or go to the gym once in a while."

"Have you thought of dancing?" I asked.

"Fat chance," Phil said. "Esther signed us up for dance lessons for our fifth anniversary, then refused to go back after the third lesson, when she saw I was hopeless."

"Not that kind of dance," I said, "although if you didn't succeed at one form, perhaps you might have tried a different style." I paused until I had their attention. "The kind I'm talking about is where you take time at the start of each day to **D.A.N.C.E.** It's what you do when you feel overwhelmed, uncomfortable, and disconnected. **D** means you determine your level of discomfort. **A** means you acknowledge your emotions by name. **N** means you name the part of your body where you feel sensations. **C** means you clarify your thoughts. **E** means you embrace the resources you have available."

"So," Phil said, "you're saying that if we can do these five things, we might be able to get in step with each other again and reconnect. That's all there is to it?"

"You also need to gain some cultural intelligence about the real world out there," Esther said. "It's not easy being a woman in the working world, but I don't come home asking for pity as you sit in front of your screens. You need to get a life."

I flipped my binder to a page of quotes. "There are some good things on the internet, as you know, Esther. For example, you just spoke about cultural intelligence. David Thomas says, 'Culturally intelligent people have the knowledge to understand cross-cultural phenomena, the mindfulness to observe and interpret particular situations, the skills required to adopt behavior to act appropriately in a range of situations.'"[14]

"Are you trying to say that I'm the one without cultural intelligence in my marriage?" Esther asked. "I have put up with a lot from this man. What else can anyone expect from me?"

"This isn't about expectations," I said. "The quote talks about 'adopting behavior to act appropriately in a range of situations.' This is a situation that requires adopting different behavior if things are going to change."

"It would be a lot easier to change my behavior if he changed his first," Esther said. "Why don't you ask more of your questions, and we'll work on that issue at home?"

"How do you want to stay connected in everyday life?"

"Where are you getting all these questions?" Esther asked.

I held up a handout. "They're listed on this paper," I said.

"Can't we work on them at home?" she asked.

"Will you?"

"What are the questions?" Phil asked.

I handed him the sheet. "Why don't you read them out, and the two of you can decide when you'll answer them?"

Phil smiled as he examined the first question.

- What do you want to do for fun?
- Where do you want to travel or what adventures do you want to have?
- What role do you want family to play in your lives?
- What do you want your social life to be like?
- If you have children, how do you want to operate together as parents?
- What do you want your home to be like?
- What do you do with your differences?
- When you find yourself in your repetitive cycle, how do you break free?
- What are the listening filters you want to use?
- How would you like your health to look?
- What do you do when at least one of you is triggered?
- How do you want to grow together?
- What do you want your physical intimacy to look like?
- How do you want to be of service to others?[15]

"That's a lot of personal stuff," Esther said. "I don't have much free time with all the demands on me already."

I accepted the paper back from Phil. "Once upon a time you built a love story that brought you together. Do you remember that story? These questions are trying to take that foundation and build something that will last. When you answer these questions, you'll discover a little more of who you brought into this relationship. Understanding who you are and who you married is crucial if we're going to move ahead together."

"Okay, but do we have to do it on our date night?" Esther asked.

"You can do it anytime you want," I said. "You just have to schedule it, and then stick to the schedule."

"We can do that," Esther said, rising to gather her coat and heading toward the door.

Phil accepted the paper from me and followed his wife toward the exit.

IDENTITY AND PERSONALITIES

> **"You can't stay in your corner of the forest waiting for others to come to you. You have to go to them sometimes."** —Winnie the Pooh

Hailey and Simon almost bounced into the office. Hailey glanced quickly out the window and then backed away, turning toward the Latin American instruments on display. Simon swerved to the bookshelf and scanned my titles. In our pre-call forms, we had highlighted the issue of identity for them as well. Both were counselors, and into personality tests, so their approach to identity stemmed from yet another angle. We had focused on the MBTI (Myers-Briggs Temperament Indicators) and had a fun time analyzing the results. At the start of our time together, I handed over their results but asked them to keep them hidden.

We first reviewed the sixteen types.

"I know you've looked at these tests before," I said. "It's important to think through what each letter stands for. The first letter in your type will be an **I** for introvert or an **E** for extrovert. All that stands for is the way you best renew your energy. If you are an **I**, you renew your energy more from alone time. You likely have a few good friends but find that large groups and events take a lot of energy from you."

"That would be me," Hailey said. "It drives me crazy when Simon wants to fill the house with bodies all the time. Girls are bopping around, saying Simon is 'Rizz' and 'authentic,' and I'm 'nice.' As in boring."

"If you are an **E**," I said, "you are labeled an extrovert. An extrovert tends to have a lot of relationships and loves to gain energy through larger groups and events."

"That's me," Simon said. "It's nice to know it's wired into me. I think Hailey thinks I'm out to drive her crazy with all the relationships I try to keep in touch with. It seems I'm always on the phone or wanting to go out somewhere."

"You can see why personality styles can be a point of conflict when it comes to identity. The next letter in your type stands for the way you take in information. If you are an **S**, it means that you take in information through your senses. You need to see it, feel it, taste it, smell it, or hear it to process it clearly. If you are an **N**, you tend to process things through your intuition. Your intuition is highly developed, and your decisions are fairly accurate most of the time."

"I'd say Hailey might be an **N** or an **S**," Simon said. "I'm not always sure how she knows things, but she's usually right about the character or motive of someone we are dealing with. I think I probably am an **S**. I need to see evidence right in front of my nose to figure out what's going on."

"We'll find out in a moment," I said. "The next letters talk about the way you make decisions. A person with the **F** makes decisions through feelings, their feelings and the feelings of others in the room. A person with a **T** tends to be logical and want to make rational choices."

"I don't even have to be logical to figure this one out," Hailey said. "Simon is so soft hearted; he is one huge ball of feelings. I can see exactly what needs to be done in a minute, and he spends hours thinking through how this is going to affect everyone's feelings along the way."

"Remember, these are not good or bad," I said. "These are tendencies we have. Some of us have these tendencies strongly, and some not so strongly. The final letter in our type is a **J** or a **P**. The **J** indicates that we like to act by having everything in order, getting it done on time and completing our tasks well. The **P** means that we like to keep our options open as long as possible, and to take in as much information as possible. It may mean getting our projects done late, but it will probably still get done well."

Hailey chuckled. "If **P** is another word for procrastinator, then you have Simon pegged. If we're doing a joint event, I'll have my part done days in advance, while he's still scrambling at the last minute. Somehow he pulls it off, and hardly anyone in the audience realizes I'm having a heart attack behind the scenes."

"Let's read through the sixteen types and see where the potential clash points might be. First, let's look at the Introverts to see if we find Hailey there. Simon, why don't you read through these?"

Sixteen Personality Types

ISTJ The Inspector is reliable and resourceful, calm under pressure and well organized. They value honor and are trustworthy. They value time and are efficient, tidy, and respectful. They keep things running smoothly.

ISFP The Artist prefers to work alone, is down-to-earth, and is usually personable and charming. They are creative, spontaneous, and cheerful. They are perfectionistic but are usually calming and can be good collaborators.

ISFJ The Defender is reserved and careful in word and action. They are highly organized, work for systemization, focus on detail, notice small things, and are clear in their expectations. They are concerned about the needs of others—enough so that they may bypass their own needs. They are punctual, caring, and work without complaint.

ISTP The Craftsman is technically intelligent. They are independent, value their own ideas most, like to do their own thing, and are effective in finding solutions and executing them quickly. They like to get things accomplished and enjoy a challenge without being micromanaged.

INTP The Thinker is extremely reserved but has an incredible imagination. They excel in abstract thought, are logical, and are strong problem solvers. They spot solutions quickly and have a wide range of knowledge, which can show up with multiple solutions. They are direct and honest in communication but like to keep options open.

INFJ The Counselor is a seeker of meaning and loves to dig deeper. They are creative, encouraging, empathetic, and supportive. They focus on others and help others feel valued and empowered.

INTJ The Mastermind is quiet and reserved but tends to be more rigid in their decision making. They look for the most efficient solutions and act on them. They solve the problems others avoid and strive to understand why things are the way they are. They are direct and to the point, while keeping high standards. They value knowledge, competence, and excellence.

INFP The Mediator is introverted and intuitive, which makes them idealists who focus on improving the world and the environment around them. They have everyone's best interest at heart, are creative, and perform well alone. They prefer a few close friendships but see the big picture and are visionaries who believe in their ability to make the world a better place."

Simon set down his sheet, furrowing his brow.

"Any guesses?" I asked.

"I think so," he answered, "but I want to wait until we're finished to be sure."

"Okay. Hailey, your turn. Why don't you read through the extroverts to see if you can guess which one best labels Simon.?"

Hailey laid the sheet down on the desk, flattened it with the palms of her hands, and read.

ENFJ The Teacher is a creative, free-thinking giver who is highly driven. You always know where they stand because of their strong ethical code and their natural ability to lead with empathy. They are intuitive, organized, confident, and genuinely concerned about the greater good. They work to help others succeed and are contagious in their enthusiasm.

ESFP The Performer is a natural entertainer, especially in the home. They are generous, friendly, curious, and approachable. They are liked by most and are enthusiastic, encouraging, and positive.

ENFP The Champion is also an energetic and creative adventurer interested in a variety of hobbies. They are inclusive and are champions of others. They are great to share ideas with and will give the feedback you need.

ENTJ The Commander is a logical, rational, and future-focused leader. They are autonomous, assertive, and confident, especially in their decision-making. They naturally take the lead and keep others in line by ensuring everyone knows their tasks and sticks with the plan.

ENTP The Visionary is logical and skilled at problem-solving because they are always looking toward the future. They are filled with big ideas. Nothing seems impossible, and while not great at following up on the details of a plan, they create the initial vision. They solve problems with imagination and can provide fun and innovation.

ESFJ The Provider is a true caregiver who's concerned with the emotional well-being of everyone around them. They work well in groups and are fun to be around. They focus on the here and now but operate firmly within rules and structures. They work best in face-to-face settings due to their skilled communication ability.

ESTP The Doer arrives like a whirlwind with no time to waste. They are creative, enthusiastic, and focused, and thrive in fluctuating group environments. They are quick to pivot when necessary but may overlook rules and procedures if they get in the way of the end goal. They like to keep things easy and efficient.

ESTJ The Supervisor is the typical Type A personality who likes to be in control. They are dedicated, organized, and dignified, and they rarely break the rules. They have a strong work ethic and work well with clear instructions or procedures. They do exactly what is requested, and they do so with outstanding character and reliability. They have strong discipline and do the right thing in the right way.[16]

Hailey was smiling as we finished. "I know exactly which one Simon is. In fact, I can see most of the youth we deal with somewhere in this."

"And I can see your type loud and clear," Simon said.

I laid out the handout and held up both hands. "Before you get into guessing anything, remember that these indicators only show us our tendencies. Every one of us is unique, even if we might share the same type. I am assuming you two aren't the same type."

"Simon is definitely a Performer, a Doer, or a Supervisor," Hailey blurted out. "Most people like him. He's an entertainer—a one-man show. He loves change in a group setting and has no problem ignoring a few rules here and there. He also likes to be in control."

"Thought you had me pegged?" Simon said. "That's a lot of leeway. I'm thinking you are either a Thinker or a Mastermind. You have an incredible imagination, and you figure out solutions to problems quickly. You're also direct and to the point."

We were all smiling. "While no two of us carry the tendencies of these types in exactly the same way," I said, "it can help us understand where our natural comfort levels flow and help with our discussions on how we will make choices as a leadership couple. So, let's have the big reveal."

Simon held up his results. "ESFP. Performer is right. I do love a good crowd, which is why it's easy to have so many of these youth in our house."

Hailey flipped over her page. "INTP. Thinker. Seems we know each other well."

"So, let me see if I can guess where your strengths and challenges are," I said. "Hailey's troubleshooting skills make her great with at-risk youth. She is always searching for the reasons behind why the youth act as they do. She loves to analyze, question, and learn about sophisticated models and theories. The problem starts when she tries this with Simon, who prefers to live in the present moment. He brings the fun for the youth and naturally connects and stimulates the party. He is a risk-taker who often jumps into situations without thinking through the facts or consequences. He finds it easy to leave Hailey to her overthinking while he entertains the youth."

"Nailed it," Hailey said. "So how do we manage our conflicts?"

"Appreciating the differences is always a good start," I said. "Simon can take Hailey's abstract ideas and make them into something practical. Hailey understands the big picture of the chaos you are in and can bring clarity to what is happening below the surface. Establishing boundaries, scheduling alone time without the youth, reflective listening during date nights, and reviewing the current realities flowing around you will help get you grounded."

"Sounds like a lot of work," Simon said. "Where do we start?"

"That's your work for this week," I said. "Take a look at who you are and who your spouse is. Write down the strengths—the things you appreciate about your spouse—and strategize on how you can work together within your types.[17] We'll sort out all the other issues at another session."

IDENTITY AND FRIENDSHIP

"Any day spent with you is my favorite day. So, today is my new favorite day." —Winnie the Pooh

Ben and Susan stopped at the entrance and peered in as if they were stepping into a lion's den. I gestured toward the loveseat and waited. They too had dipped their toes into the water of this identity quagmire. The tension of Ben's duet with the worship leader had lessened, but even after such a great start, there was still a need for more discussion and clarity about who they were.

Susan unloaded first. "We both left our careers to serve together as a team. We left it all and got through our training. We had huge visions and goals, and we used to dream together so much. Then the kids started coming. He kept going to school, the savings almost ran out, and we jumped into a church plant. I feel like he's getting all the glory up front, and I'm getting the dirty diapers. And now, he's all googly-eyes with the worship leader."

Ben shifted uncomfortably on the loveseat where they sat. "We can't be the only ones who have messed up. What's your story?"

I leaned back in my chair. "So, you want to get personal, do you? After eighteen years of high-paced ministry in Kenya, I returned to Canada to step into a senior role whose mandate was recouping a congregation that was scheduled for shutdown. At the time, I was fueled by two thoughts in my head. The first came from a book I'd read. It said that no one over forty-four could succeed at this task due to the amount of time and energy it required. The second I'd heard from a seminary professor, who postulated that if you slept more than four hours a night, you were wasting your life. I put those ideas to work and paid the personal price to achieve success. When others reined back their efforts, I reframed reality in terms of personal capacity."

"Sounds like you were worse off than we are."

"I had to learn two things to find my balance," I said. "I'll tell you one of them. I learned to say that there is only one Savior and it's not me. Whenever I met with people, I said these words right at the beginning of our time together. The other thing I'll leave for another session."

"So, you're telling us that you learned who you were, and who you weren't."

"Yes!"

"What do other leaders do?" Susan asked.

I reached toward my bookshelf and pulled off a volume. "Carey Nieuwhof hasn't been shy about declaring the depression he sank into after ten years of running at an unsustainable pace. His sixty to eighty hours a week stoked his pride and arrogance as his church grew. Demands will always outgrow energy. He says he is convinced that most leaders operate with low-grade burnout which can definitely be a source of conflict.[18] A lot of leaders I meet go full out and hit burnout, exhaustion, or depression before they realize what's happening. They're moving, but more like a car with flat tires."

"Been there, done that," Susan said.

I reached for another book called *The Emotionally Healthy Leader*. "Pete Scazzero says that 'unhealthy leaders engage in more activities than their combined spiritual, physical, and emotional reserves can sustain… The demands and pressures of leadership make it nearly impossible for them to establish a consistent and sustainable rhythm of life.'"[19]

"Sounds right," Ben said.

"The impact on your closest relationship is seen by others, often before you notice anything. Understanding who you are and who you aren't is crucial to building up the reserves needed for you, for your partner, and for the ministry. It's also important to realize who your partner is and who they aren't."

"I'm getting that message," Ben said.

I reached for one more book. "Loritts postulates that the leader with a lasting influence will be marked by brokenness, communion, servanthood, and obedience.[20] You are unique, but the convictions arising from your sense of identity impact whether you try to be someone you're not. It will inform how you compare yourself to others, how you cover up your insecurities, how you define and manage your fears and values— in your interactions with others, as well as your spouse."

"Keep talking," Susan prompted.

"Leaders have blind spots, and your identity can determine what those might be. These will determine your sense of self-awareness, your self-interest, and your acts of self-protection. Whether you can collaborate fully or not will be impacted by the identities you place on others and the ones you think they place on you. As Warren Bennis said, 'Becoming a leader is synonymous with becoming yourself. It is precisely that simple. And it is also that difficult.'"[21]

"Looks like I've got to spend a little more time at home with you," Ben said, looking deeply into Susan's eyes. She squeezed his hand and gazed back.

I continued. "One of the key things we want to address as we wrestle with identity is whether our partner is accessible, responsive, and engaged with who we are. Relationship guru, John Gottman, has done research around this."

The determining factor in whether wives feel satisfied with the sex, romance, and passion in their marriage is, by seventy percent, the quality of the couple's friendship. For men, the determining factor is, by seventy percent, the quality of the couple's friendship. So men and women come from the same planet after all.[22]

"I think we can pull off the friendship thing," Ben said.

I pressed on. "Friendship implies a mutual respect and an enjoyment of each other's company. It requires an understanding of your partner's quirks and idiosyncrasies, likes and dislikes, and hopes and dreams—all the while exhibiting an expressed fondness for your most valuable relationship."

"I sure wouldn't mind less fighting," Susan said.

We weren't done. "If your measurement of a happy marriage includes less conflict, it may surprise you to know that it isn't the number of issues you engage with, but whether there is good repair work done after the conflict that makes the difference. Unhappy couples get trapped in conflict and then get stuck deeper through criticism, contempt, defensiveness, and stonewalling. A couple who knows how to repair relationships realizes when it's time to stop, breathe, and find a new track for connection."

"We do get some good walks in after those fights," Ben said. "And the making up is good."

Susan blushed.

I tried to turn this session toward a conclusion. "The key to relationship is to believe that the one you love sincerely likes you, values you, and is willing to engage with you—that they recognize and affirm your positive qualities. They should be willing to put your needs ahead of theirs when it matters. All this is strengthened by following through on promises and responsibilities. Some relationship coaches focus on improving communication tools when what is needed is a stronger connection outside the point of conflict. It might be wise to set aside your point of disagreement and engage in something positive you both enjoy."

"I think we have a few of those things," Ben said.

Susan nodded as she tried to take notes on what I'd said.

"Find the good in each other and affirm it. Learn to express appreciation and gratitude. Show interest in some of the specifics your partner is engaged in. Re-establish yearly, monthly, and daily rituals to keep connected. Ask open-ended questions. Take the initiative to move toward your partner by focusing on their love language. It is a completely different experience to be in a quagmire with a friend than with someone you can't stand at that moment. If you feel your partner is trying to convict, coerce, control, or compel you in a way you don't want to respond to, then the result of your communication will not be what you had hoped."

"You might have to repeat some of that," Susan said.

I held out a handout. "I've copied most of it down. Understanding as much as we can about who we are, and who we are married to, can ease the tensions caused by lack of knowledge. Getting to know each other takes time and commitment and intentional investment. Anthony Kiedis says being secure in our identity keeps us from unhealthy ambition, frees us to learn from criticism, helps us enjoy times of restoration, and strengthens us for confrontation."[23]

Susan nodded as she scanned the handout. "I think I'm going to have to take some time to absorb all that."

"Just remember this," I said. "All humans are valuable because they are created in the image of God. Every person on the planet has needs and values, and they deserve dignity and respect. Every one of us is unique with our own personality, gifts, experiences, and dreams, and we see the world differently. This means both of you have been shaped exactly as God wanted, for a specific purpose. Let's start there."

IDENTITY AND RESPONSIBILITY

"Emotionally healthy leaders see their emotions as invitations, not obstacles to the mission of God."[24]
—Pete Scazzero

Francis and Nyota slipped into the office like children on their first day of school. They examined the artifacts sitting on the shelves, glanced out the window, ran their fingers over the love seat, and settled on the two cushioned chairs near my desk. Francis spotted the clock on the wall and then adjusted his wristwatch to sync with it. Nyota sluffed off her coat and sat ready for the lesson.

"I see you're ready for something special," I said. "Did you get your goals sorted out for what you'd like to see in our times together?"

Francis shoulder-checked to see if Nyota was ready to speak, and when he saw her arms folded and her mouth clamped shut, he took the lead. "I think we need to examine why we react the way we do. The way we grew up probably has something do with who we think we are and how we respond to each other. We tend to blame each other and not take responsibility for what we do."

"Speak for yourself," Nyota said. "I'm here to figure out why he gets hyper every time I step out the door without leaving him a note."

I reached onto my bookshelf and held out a volume. "Have you ever read *Emotionally Healthy Spirituality*?"[25] When both shook their heads, I opened the book. "Chapter seven talks about the new skills we need in order to love well. It says we can have significant positions in our ministry but be emotionally unprepared for the relationships we live in. It takes special skills to grow into an emotionally mature adult."

"Are you saying that to him or to me?" Nyota asked.

"I'm just saying. I want to show you a handout and see if you can identify your emotional identity from what is listed." I slid a copy of the handout across the desk to each of them, and they spent a moment scanning it. "Let's read it one section at a time. Francis, why don't you go first?"

"Traits of Emotional Infants. Are you trying to tell me something?" He waited, and when I didn't respond, he continued.

- They look for others to take care of them.
- They have great difficulty entering the world of others.
- They are driven by need for instant gratification.
- They use others as objects to meet their needs.

"That's him all right," Nyota said. "I walk away for an hour, and he's panicking as if he can't cope. He was never this way when we met. He's so gifted in what he does. People almost worship the ground he walks on. You'd never guess he was so helpless behind the scenes."

"Thanks for your unbiased opinion," Francis said. "I'm not that way all the time. And it's not as if you're never like that."

"Okay, remember ground rules," I said. "Dignity and respect. Positive encouragement. You're a team. We're here to move forward, together. Nyota, please read the next section."

Nyota straightened her back, set her shoulders, and read with clear enunciation. "Traits of Emotional Children:"

- They are content and happy as long as they receive what they want.
- They unravel quickly from stress, disappointments, and trials.
- They interpret disagreements as personal offenses.
- They are easily hurt.
- They complain, withdraw, manipulate, take revenge, and become sarcastic when they don't get their way.
- They have great difficulty calmly discussing their needs and wants in a mature, loving way.

"Well, well, well," Francis said. "I'm positive I recognize some of these traits, and I respect the character of the one who is willing to admit it." He smirked, before hiding his face behind the handout. "Ok, I've got the next one. Traits of Emotional Adolescents:"

- They tend to be defensive.
- They are threatened and alarmed by criticism.
- They keep score of what they give so they can ask for something later in return.
- They deal with conflict poorly, often blaming, appeasing, going to a third party, pouting, or ignoring the issue entirely.
- They become preoccupied with themselves.

- They have great difficulty truly listening to another person's pain, disappointments, or needs.
- They are critical and judgmental.

Nyota smiled as she retook her position. "Traits of Emotional Adults. Finally."

- They can ask for what they need, want, or prefer—clearly, directly, honestly.
- "They recognize, manage, and take responsibility for their own thoughts and feelings.
- They can, when under stress, state their own beliefs and values without becoming adversarial.
- They respect others without having to change them.
- They give people room to make mistakes and not be perfect.
- They appreciate people for who they are—the good, bad, and ugly—not for what they give back.
- They accurately assess their own limits, strengths, and weaknesses and can freely discuss them with others.
- They are deeply in tune with their own emotional world and able to enter into the feelings, needs, and concerns of others without losing themselves.
- They have capacity to resolve conflict maturely and negotiate solutions that consider the perspective of others."

"I don't expect you to determine exactly which one is your identity right now," I said. "I just want you to realize that the skill and ability you show in your ministry may be far different than the skill and maturity you display in your emotional relationships. That may be one reason you get into these unexpected clashes."

"You know I'm not into psychobabble, doc," Francis said. "Just give it to us straight. Are you saying that the way our families treated us is somehow still impacting us now, even though we're adults? That somewhere along the way, we got stuck and didn't grow up?"

"Is that what you noticed from what you saw on this list?" I asked.

"It's hard to miss that," Nyota said.

"Okay, if that's what happened along the way, how do you think that might be affecting your marriage relationship?"

Francis put his handout back on the desk. "It means we have to grow up somehow. We have to figure out who we are now—and who we want to be—and then how to get from here to there."

"And how would you go about getting from here to there?" I asked. "Where would you start?"

"When I look at this list," Francis said, "I can see that there are a few things in one list that are me and a few in another. How do you explain that?"

"It means you've matured in some areas faster than others. It also means that there are some relationships, some situations, and some times of the year that hit us differently and draw out parts of us we didn't realize were there."

"You make us sound like we have multiple personalities or something," Nyota said.

"Oh, you're all one person, and that's what makes this all so confusing," I said. "You are one person fluctuating between different emotional stages at different times with different people."

I shelved the book I'd been using. "Have you ever returned to a family reunion with all your siblings and found yourself slipping back into an old role, an old feeling, or an old personality? Everything works fine if everyone plays their role, but if you start bringing in outsiders who know a different side of you, it can make things awkward and confusing for those who knew you from before and those who know you now."

"How does that work in our marriage?" Nyota asked.

"If you met Francis in a professional setting and got to know him for who he was then, it can be surprising to encounter another side of him you didn't expect. Like you said, when he's in front of people, he is skilled, and people almost worship the ground he walks on. You go away without leaving a note, and suddenly he's a helpless child ready to throw a tantrum because you're not taking care of him."

"So," Nyota said, "you're saying that when it comes to identity, we're pretty complex if we're not paying attention."

"And that's why we have to take responsibility for ourselves," I said. I leafed through my binder. "One more handout to read. Taking responsibility is a key pillar of a thriving relationship. When we blame each other without understanding what's under the surface, we end up creating suffering and disconnection. If you can approach your conversations, taking one hundred percent responsibility, it brings about a freedom we can hardly imagine."

"You want me to read this?" Nyota asked.

"We're going to alternate again," I said. "Read both lines. First, the one that sounds like blame and then the one that sounds like responsibility. Francis, you're up!"

Francis smiled. "When we want to Blame, it sounds like: you're not listening to me. When we take Responsibility, it sounds like: I wonder how I can communicate in a way that makes it easier to hear me?"

"I'm going to like this exercise," Nyota said. "Blame: you don't communicate with me. Responsibility: I wonder how I can listen in a way that makes it easier, safer, or more inviting to want to openly share yourself with me."

"I see," Francis said. "When we're blaming, we start with 'you this' and 'you that.' When we're taking responsibility, we start with 'I wonder.'"

"You got it! Now take those sheets home and see if you can read through the rest of the list. Practice these once a day on your own and see if it helps adjust your thinking. If you can adjust your thinking, you'll be amazed by how it affects your understanding— of your own identity as well as your partner's."

QUAGMIRE TWO

Attachment

**"We are never more emotional
than when our primary love relationship is threatened."**[26]
—Sue Johnson

Any study in relationship these days passes through the territory
of attachment. Once considered an issue relegated to parents and
their children, it is now considered a fundamental truth that a drive to
emotionally attach to a safe, secure person is hardwired into our genes.
"Loving contact is as important as physical nutrition."[27]

Ministry and marriage come into conflict when our safety and security are rooted in our ministry more than our marriage—especially
when we don't feel those things in our primary relationship. If a marital
relationship struggles, it is not always the conflict between ministry and
marriage that's recognized as the cause. Now we understand that "de-
creasing affection and emotional responsiveness" is our best predictor for
what lies ahead for a couple. [28]

When we think about attachment, we want to consider the impact
of our relationship, our feelings, and the cycles of communication we
repeat. We also want to consider raw spots, forgiveness, the stories we
tell ourselves, and the source of panic that stretches our connection.

In a coaching relationship, the aim is to work toward hope, transparent communication, and common goals and values. The coach acts
as a neutral support, providing feedback and functioning like a mirror
to reflect what is there and what needs attention. Both partners should

feel heard and understood. Fears and frustrations can be aired and sifted for underlying realities. Emotional pains can be identified and recurring patterns adjusted so that the needs of both partners are met.

ATTACHMENT AND RELATIONSHIP

> **"Being able to declare our core attachment fears naturally leads to a recognition of our primary attachment needs. Fear and longing are two sides of the same coin."**[29] —Sue Johnson

Sam and Hannah arrived fifteen minutes late to their next session. He held the door for her, but it was clear she wasn't ready to give him credit for any gestures. She flung her coat down on the loveseat and stood behind it. "The sitter was late. Sam forgot to call me. I took a taxi. We're here."

"How did it make you feel to be forgotten?" I asked.

"Oh, don't worry about me. I'm used to it," Hannah answered. "Sam sits under a toxic board that treats him like his own parents did. He bows to their every demand and leaves me to fend for myself."

"That must be difficult," I said, motioning toward the loveseat. "Sam, feel free to have a seat."

"That's okay, I'll stand," he said.

"It sounds like we need to talk about the issue of attachment. Perhaps you'd feel comfortable standing by my desk so you can look at a couple of handouts." Sam moved closer, but Hannah leaned over the loveseat and strained to see from there. "If you've ever listened to a mother talk to her frightened child, you might notice that she speaks softly and slowly, trying to comfort her little one in a low voice. She is assuring the child that she's there in the middle of what they are experiencing and that things are going to be okay. As adults, we can't always avoid the painful moments, but we can bring our full presence into the core of what our partner is facing so they don't have to deal with it alone. Our voice and our body language speak loudly about our willingness to be present for our partner."

"I read something about that in *Created for Connection*,"[30] Hannah said. "This has something to do with the amygdala, the emotional part of our brain. When we feel secure, we connect easily, and when we don't, we get anxious or controlling or something like that."

"Well done!" I said. "Having a safe haven to go to gives us strength and confidence. We feel vulnerable and disoriented when that safe haven seems out of reach. As you said, we become more demanding and controlling because we're desperate to reattach and feel secure again. Sometimes the demands of ministry pull us apart rather than bringing us together, and we find ourselves stuck in old patterns of attachment without knowing why."

"The book also talks about how the patterns of our early attachments can impact our current attachments," Sam said. "I think Hannah's family situation is having a big impact on us right now. Her parents split when she was young, so she thinks that's a viable option for her when things get tough. I can't live with that kind of insecurity."

"The issue is that you're controlling, like my father," Hannah said. "You think that creating rules will solve all our problems. I can tell you it's not working for the kids, and it's not working for me."

I pushed the handouts across the desk. "You may remember that there are four different attachment styles. If your primary caretaker made you feel safe as a youngster, you might have grown into a self-confident and trusting individual. You might be more hopeful, responsive, and positive. If you experienced confusion, fear, or inconsistent emotional communication as a child, you likely have trouble navigating emotions—your own as well as the feelings of those around you. You might be clingy or anxious in your bonding. Perhaps you can find your style on this paper, and then we can examine whether it applies to your own relationship. Take a look at the first style. Hannah, perhaps you can read through it."

"I know that's not all we have to think about," Hannah said, walking around the loveseat to pick up the handout. "I was impacted not only by my parents splitting up, but by an abusive uncle, a babysitter, and a lot of bad dates."

"The important thing to realize is that you're not trapped by whatever attachment style you have," I said. "Your brain is amazingly adaptable, and we can learn to make and develop new patterns of response. Hannah, you can see the four styles of attachment: secure, ambivalent, avoidant-dismissive, and disorganized.[31] Please read the secure attachment, and let me know if that's what you experience."

"Secure attachment style. Someone who is securely attached will

- be empathetic;
- set appropriate boundaries;
- be stable, safe, and satisfied through their feelings in close relationships;
- thrive in close, meaningful relationships;
- be willing to take responsibility for their own mistakes and failings;
- seek help and support when they need it;
- be themself in an intimate relationship;
- comfortably express their feelings, hopes, and needs;
- find satisfaction in being with others;
- not get overly anxious when they and their partner are apart;
- openly seek support when they need it, and welcome the chance to support;
- maintain emotional balance and manage conflict in healthy ways;
- bounce back with resilience: from disappointments, setbacks, and misfortune."

Hannah scanned the list again. "Okay, less than half of this list applies to me."

Sam cleared his throat and set the paper on the desk before sitting back on the loveseat. "Can't say I relate with too many of these things at home, but it makes sense at work."

I nodded to Sam. "Would you read the next style, please?"

Ambivalent or anxious-preoccupied attachment style. A person with this style

- is overly needy, anxious, uncertain, and lacking in self-esteem;
- craves emotional intimacy, but worries that others don't want to be with them;
- might be embarrassed by clinginess or constant need for love and attention;
- might feel worn down by anxiety over their partner's commitment and love;
- struggles to feel that they can trust and fully rely on their partner;
- becomes overly fixated on the partner they desire for an intimate relationship;
- has difficulty with boundaries, and considers space between themself and their partner as a source for panic, anger, or fear;
- overreacts to threats to the relationship since self-worth rests on how they feel they're being treated by their partner;
- feels anxious or jealous when away from their partner and might use guilt, controlling behavior, or other manipulation to keep them closer;
- needs constant reassurance and lots of attention from their partner;
- may encounter criticism from others who label them as too clingy or needy.

Sam nodded. "I can see myself in some of this, although I don't like to admit it. I don't think it's fair to blame my mom or dad on how I interact with Hannah."

"I'll read the next one," Hannah said.

"Avoidant-dismissive attachment style. A person with this style may

- feel wary of closeness and try to avoid emotional connection with others;
- hesitate to rely on others or have others rely on them;
- find it difficult to tolerate emotional intimacy;
- value independence and freedom to the point they feel stifled by closeness;

- be independent and prefer to care for themselves, feeling no need of others;
- withdraw more and more, the closer or needier a partner becomes;
- be accused of being distant, closed off, uncomfortable with emotions, rigid, or intolerant;
- accuse a partner of being too needy;
- be quick to minimize or disregard the feelings of their partner—keeping secrets from them, exploring other relationships, and even ending relationships to regain a sense of freedom;
- focus on casual relationships over long-term intimate ones, or embrace equally independent partners who remain emotionally distant."

Hannah glanced up and fixed her glare on me. "Did you have me read this one for a reason?"

"Does it apply?" I asked.

She nodded. "Big time. How can we rewire our brains if our caregivers were emotionally withdrawn from us? I've learned to self-soothe because I'm the only one I can count on to be there for me. And now, Sam is repeating the cycle all over again by not being around."

Sam raised his hand. "I'll read the last one. Maybe this one is more like me."

Disorganized-disoriented (fearful-avoidant) attachment style. A person with this style may be

- fearful, based on childhood trauma, neglect, or abuse;
- feeling like they don't deserve love or closeness;
- unable to self-soothe their emotions, causing other relationships to feel unsafe;
- replicating their childhood abuse in their adult relationships;
- finding intimate relationships confusing and unsettling, swinging between love and hate;

- insensitive towards their partner—selfish, controlling, and untrusting—which can lead to explosive or abusive behavior;
- as hard on themselves as on others;
- antisocial or negative in their behavior patterns;
- abusing drugs or alcohol or prone to aggression and violence;
- refusing to take responsibility for their actions;
- feeling unworthy of love and terrified of getting hurt again.

Sam shook his head. "Nope. Not that one. This sounds like my older sister. My mom was an unwed teen when my sister was born, and Mom didn't handle life too well in those days. I think she had been on drugs or something. My sister says that my grandparents kicked her out of the house, and she was depressed and on the streets for a few months before she met my dad and eventually got married. By the time I was born, things were better, but not great."

"Okay, so we're both messed up," Hannah said. "Where do we go from here?"

"Coming here is a good start," I said. "We can work on our nonverbal skills, since some of the body language—like your gestures, postures, facial expressions, and eye contact—may be saying things you don't really mean. You might also be reading into signals that your partner isn't meaning to send."

"Like, when I walked in the door and threw my coat on the love seat," Hannah said. "What if I'm sending signals, and he is just not getting them?"

"We can work on those as well," I said. "You could elevate your emotional intelligence, which means you can learn to understand, use, and manage your emotions in more positive ways so you can empathize, handle conflict, and communicate more effectively."

"We don't always do well at communicating our needs and feelings," Sam acknowledged.

Both Sam and Hannah backed up and sat side by side in the loveseat. "Another thing you could do is to develop healthy relationships with people who are doing relationship right. They are securely attached and know how to think and behave in a positive way. Believe it or not, more than half of all relationships are secure and healthy enough for you to gain support from them. A strong friendship with a healthy couple will help provide guardrails and roadmaps when you feel like you're struggling."

"I'm not sure if any of this will work until I sort out my childhood trauma," Hannah said. "I think Sam might use some help as well before we get back together and rub each other raw."

"We've got to figure out how to care for the kids better while all this adjustment is going on," Sam said. "I'm not the best one to care for them on my own."

"Perhaps you can go on a few walks over the next week and talk that through," I suggested.

"Perhaps you can identify a couple who would walk alongside you and function as an anchor until you stabilize."

Sam rose. "Looks like we've got our work cut out for us."

Attachment and Feelings

> **"The truth is that emotions never die. They are only buried alive. They always resurface, leaking into other parts of our lives and relationships."[32] —Sue Johnson**

Jim and Sharon arrived five minutes early, and Sharon poked her head in the door as I was finishing up a report from my last client. "Is it okay to come in?" she asked.

I pointed toward the love seat and signed off on my paperwork. "Nice to see you two eager for some focus on attachment. How did the walk and talk go this week?"

Jim shut the door behind them and made his trip to the water cooler. "We did get our walk in, if that's what you're asking. We were wondering if you had some way to measure how we're doing?"

"What do you mean by that?" I asked.

"You know," he answered. "How are we doing at being safe and attached? Friends of ours thought it was strange that we were focusing on so much to do with emotion."

I flipped open my binder and slipped out two handouts. "Once upon a time, some of our western cultures used to think that healthy mature adults didn't need emotional connection. In this line of thinking, we should be fully sufficient on our own. If we needed someone, we were labeled as dysfunctional, codependent, enmeshed, too emotional, and too needy. Therapists in the past spent a lot of time trying to get us to stand on our own."

"That's exactly what happened to me after our first year of marriage," Sharon said. "I was told I was too needy and too emotional. I'm sure the guy used that word—codependent."

"Sorry to hear that," I said. "Every human has this basic need for connection. It's part of our mental, emotional, and even spiritual health. It's part of your creation." Sharon reached for the two sheets of paper and passed one to her husband, so I continued. "Our conflict comes when there is an absence of intimate interactions with the one we are connected to. You might think you're fighting about the kids, your intimacy, or a calendar conflict, but there's something else going on behind the scenes."

"So, this test is supposed to solve our calendar conflict?" Jim asked.

"No, in every conflict, we're asking some basic questions. Questions like 'Can I count on you?' 'Are you there for me?' 'Will you respond to me when I need you?' 'Do I matter to you?' 'Am I valued and accepted by you?' and 'Do you need me?'"

"So, you're saying that what we're fighting about is not really the issue we're fighting about," Sharon said.

"You got it! Your anger, criticism, withdrawal, demands, and reactions are all attempts to draw attention to unmet needs— an attempt to warn you about a feeling of disconnection. Your reactions are a cry to your partner that they need to pay attention and re-establish a safe connection."

"I knew there was something more going on," Sharon said. "I thought it might be just a woman thing. You know how they say women need relationships more? If it's a human thing, then I feel more of a right to let Jim know what I'm feeling. It's my attempt to make him love me."

Jim crossed his legs and glanced at the paper. "I guess if you don't ask, you don't get," he said.

"That may be true," I said, "but Sharon needs to feel that it is safe, and okay, to ask. That's what this test is about. Let's take a few minutes and fill the form out as honestly as you can."

THE A.R.E. QUESTIONNAIRE.

From your viewpoint, is your partner accessible to you?

1. I can get my partner's attention easily. (T/F)
2. My partner is easy to connect with emotionally. (T/F)
3. My partner shows me that I come first with him/her. (T/F)
4. I am not feeling lonely or shut out in this relationship. (T/F)
5. I can share my deepest feelings with my partner. He/she will listen. (T/F)

From your viewpoint, is your partner responsive to you?

1. If I need connection and comfort, he/she will be there for me. (T/F)
2. My partner responds to signals that I need him/her to come close. (T/F)
3. I find I can lean on my partner when I am anxious or unsure. (T/F)
4. Even when we fight or disagree, I know that I am important to my partner, and we will find a way to come together. (T/F)
5. If I need reassurance about how important I am to my partner, I can get it. (T/F)

Are you positively emotionally engaged with each other?

1. I feel very comfortable being close to and trusting my partner. (T/F)
2. I can confide in my partner about almost anything. (T/F)
3. I feel confident, even when we are apart, that we are connected to each other. (T/F)

4. I know that my partner cares about my joys, hurts, and fears. (T/F)

5. I feel safe enough to take emotional risks with my partner. (T/F)[33]

"When you're finished, we'll process the results," I said after ten minutes.

"This issue of emotions is unfamiliar territory for me," Jim said. "Do you have any way to help me make sense of it? If I'm supposed to be emotionally aware of what Susan is going through, I may need a map of some kind."

I flipped a few more pages in my binder and pulled out another sheet. On the paper was a large colored circle entitled "The Emotions Circle."

"Emotions say a lot about what is going on inside in terms of our thinking," I said. "You may see Sharon's body language and assume you know what's going on, but what is happening underneath the surface may be more complex than you realize."

"Okay, I can buy that," Jim said. "What is that handout you have all about?"

I handed over the feelings wheel. "You can see that this feelings wheel has an inner circle, surrounded by a larger circle, and finally an outside circle. The inner circle is divided into seven pie shapes to represent our seven basic feelings. There is anger, fearful, bad, surprised, happy, sad, and disgusted. Each of those divide down in the second circle into parts, and those parts are divided down again in the largest circle. This chart gives you language to understand exactly what is happening inside yourself or your partner."

"Can you explain it a little better?" Sharon asked.

"Sure, let me take out one segment of the pie chart and break it down," I said. "I'll put it into a chart form." I flipped the page and drew out a chart on the back. "Let's focus on anger."

Angry	Let Down	Betrayed
		Resentful
	Humiliated	Disrespectful
		Ridiculed
	Bitter	Indignant
		Violated
	Mad	Furious
		Jealous
	Aggressive	Provoked
		Hostile
	Frustrated	Infuriated
		Annoyed
	Distant	Withdrawn
		Numb
	Critical	Sceptical
		Dismissive

"Let's assume that Sharon is still angry because you didn't tell her about the scheduled retreat on the weekend you always book for her family."

"I'm not sure we have to assume that," Jim said.

"For the sake of this exercise, take a look at the chart. In the inner circle you can see that she is angry; but do you know for sure how that is playing out inside of her? Is she feeling let down by you, humiliated before her family, bitter at another uncommunicated event, or generally mad at what this says about your relationship? Is she feeling aggressive toward you, frustrated with you, distant from you, or critical of you? Do you know?"

"Probably a lot of that," Jim said.

"You don't know unless you ask her." I turned toward Sharon. "Sharon, how would you track through this chart? Can you see how your feelings play out?"

"I've probably gone through stages," Sharon said. "I was definitely angry. Maybe let down and humiliated at first, then bitter, frustrated. Maybe distant."

"How are these playing out now?" I asked.

Sharon looked at Jim and pursed her lips. "I guess for the let down options, I felt more betrayed. For the humiliated options, I felt more disrespected. For the bitter options, I felt indignant. For the mad options, I was furious. For the frustrated options, I was infuriated. For the distant options, I felt withdrawn."

"Those are strong emotions," I said. "By giving Jim a clear path to understand what you're feeling, he can see that his attachment to you is in serious jeopardy. He needs to know that you're feeling he is not proving to be available, engaged, or responsive."

"Okay, sorry I asked about the emotions part," Jim said. "I think Sharon has made herself very clear now. How about if we look at the happy section of the chart?"

"Why don't the two of you take this home and go over it together? All the tools I give you are meant to be conversation starters."

"I guess I already know how this A.R.E. test is going to turn out," Jim said. "It's time to face the music."

Sharon patted the back of Jim's hand. "Just remember, dear, I feel so strongly because I love you. I just need to know that you're going to be there for me when I need you."

"Let's finish up with a quick mention of those needs," I said. "Every human has needs. Human needs, at their core, are fairly universal. For example, we need relationships to be honest, peaceful, meaningful, and secure. We also need time for play, autonomy, and physical well-being. How these needs are met may look different for each person in the relationship."

"You're telling Sharon that it's okay to have needs," Jim said.

"More than that. Every human has common needs. Honesty is reflected when my relationship with you has authenticity, integrity, and my full presence. Play may involve joy, humor, sabbath, and celebration."

"Some of these have a lot of parts to them," Jim interrupted.

"Yes," I said. "Look at peace. Peace may involve beauty, regular healthy connection, a sense of ease and equality, forgiveness, harmony, inspiration, and order. Autonomy may involve real choice, freedom, independence, space, or even spontaneity and uncertainty. Connection may include some of acceptance, affection, appreciation, belonging, cooperation, and strong communication. Or it may involve closeness, vibrant community, companionship, compassion, and consistency. Or it may involve empathy, inclusion, intimacy, love, mutuality, nurturing, and respect. Or it may involve support, seeing and knowing and understanding, trust, service, warmth, and time together. It's such a multifaceted need."

"Did you get a load of connection?" Jim asked. "That's like drinking from Niagara Falls."

"Take it in pieces," I said.

"You worked overseas," Sharon said. "How did your needs show up when you came back here?"

"When I first arrived back in Canada, after ministry in Kenya, I questioned how effective I could be after eighteen years anchored elsewhere. I meditated, and asked God what I needed to know on my return. He simply said, *Food. Water. Exercise. Sleep.* Twenty-five years later, I am still wrestling with the balance of food, water, exercise and sleep. Just because we know we have basic needs doesn't mean we take the steps to ensure those needs are being met."

"So, having a PhD doesn't mean you have it all together," Jim said.

"Not at all. The need for physical well-being is one thing I still struggle with. Breathing good air, eating well, regular and frequent exercise, sound sleep, healthy intimacy, safety, shelter, touch, and plenty of water. All this matters and impacts our mental and relational health."

"This need for attachment is significant," Jim said.

"Yes, but each need is about more than it appears to be. Security is a need for many in terms of certainty, safety, and stability."

"I can relate with those ones," Sharon said. "How would you break down meaning? It's another Niagara Falls."

"Let's break it into four chunks," I said. "Meaning is another need for some when it comes to awareness, affirmation, and celebration of life. Or it may involve challenge, clarity, competence, consciousness, contribution, creativity, and discovery. Or it may mean efficacy, effectiveness, significance, and growth. Or it may mean hope, learning, mourning, and participation. Or it may mean purpose, self-expression, stimulation, and understanding."[34]

"You're overwhelming me with all these options," Sharon said.

"Take your time," I responded. "These are just mirrors to look at."

"I think we're going to be busy this week, going over our needs and feelings," Jim said.

ATTACHMENT AND CYCLES

"Friendship is a sheltering tree." —Samuel Taylor Coleridge

Ben and Susan arrived, eating ice cream cones. I looked out the window at a cloudy, drizzly day. "Interesting choice for such a cool day," I said.

"It was Ben's choice for our date," Susan said. "We used to do this when we first went out, and we're trying to connect again around some of the things that brought us together."

"Sounds like a great idea," I said. "One of the realities about a secure attachment is that when you feel comfortable and confident about your closeness with each other, you'll get better at looking for and gaining the support you need. You're also open to more experiences and can better handle a diversity of opinions."

Ben swallowed and smiled. "I think Susan has been noticing that when I get busy and scattered, I become more inflexible. I don't have the capacity to manage a whole lot of change. When we have space to relax a bit, I can get a little more curious about some of the wilder things she wants to explore."

Susan nodded. "You should probably explain what you mean by wilder things, but it's true. The safer and more secure I feel about our relationship, the more independent I can be. I can sort things out on my own, and I can usually do what I need to do with the resources I have."

"One of the things couples I work with are discovering is that, because they didn't realize how essential their attachment is, they haven't been clearly communicating their needs and emotions. We get so distracted with everyday life—caught up in our own emotions and setting our own agendas." I pulled my chair forward. "So, it's not surprising that when we get into our own worlds, we forget to communicate to our best friend about a calendar issue."

Ben popped the last bit of his cone into his mouth. "I still don't know how to realize that she needs my attention and connection if she doesn't tell me."

"Good observation," I said. "Realize that we all have basic needs that have to be fulfilled and that, as the best friend and partner of our spouse, we have the unique opportunity to keep checking that those needs are being met." I took out another handout and slid it across the desk. "Take a look at this," I said.

"'Surface Feelings,'" Ben read. "What are we supposed to do with these?"

"I want you to remember how you were feeling during your last big conflict, maybe the one where you had to sort out things with Susan about your duet with the worship leader. Each of you likely had very different feelings at that moment, but the whole situation demonstrates how you communicate with each other. I'll read them out, and you circle the ones that apply."

Susan snagged a yellow highlighter off my desk, and Ben pulled a pen from his pocket. "Always work when we come here, isn't there?"

"Not as much as when you're home," I said. "Here's the list."

Anger	Exhausted	Defensive
Frustration	Fear	Cold
Disappointment	Anxious	Numb
Apathy	Hopeless	Elusive
Indifference	Tiredness	Panicked
Sadness	Annoyed	Discouraged
Overwhelmed	Irritable	

Okay, now go to the next list. In attachment theory, there are usually one of three dynamics at work. Either both of you are pursuers who are fighting to reconnect; you may see a lot of intense discussion—and even volume—if this is true. The second dynamic is where one of you is the pursuer, and the other is a withdrawer trying to avoid the confrontation; in that case, one of you might get very loud and one very quiet. In the third pattern, both of you might withdraw in order to keep the peace, and so nothing gets said out loud. This is the most dangerous pattern for the relationship. So, do you know which one you are?"

"I'm definitely the pursuer," Susan said.

"I'm the withdrawer," Ben said. "I prefer to say I'm the peacemaker."

"This list gives you a choice of what your tendency is if the first list is felt. Circle from the right section, Pursuer or Withdrawer."

Pursuer tendencies.

- You keep pursuing the conversation; become dominating, controlling, aggressive, nagging, critical.
- You become more agitated, frustrated, angry, and anxious under stress.
- You want to talk things through. You may talk excessively, interrupt, and get defensive.
- You insist on making your point.
- You complain, express your disapproval, point out your beloved's mistakes, and make requests that sound like demands.
- When your partner steps away or stops responding, you get triggered and feel rejected, alone, and unsupported.
- You pursue your partner because you keep trying to reconnect.

Withdrawer tendencies.

- You shut down, withdraw, become quiet, zone out and/or check out.
- You get flooded and overwhelmed by your partner's big emotions and insistence that you talk it through.
- You feel attacked, criticized, and on the defensive.
- You possibly justify what you do and make your partner seem wrong for how they feel.
- You stop listening and numb out.
- You stay in your head.

- You create distance.
- You refuse to talk.
- Rather than try to make it better, you give up.
- To prevent the disconnection from worsening, you talk less and step away (physically and/or emotionally) — in the hopes that you can keep the peace by withdrawing from the conflict.

"So, what's your combined list, Susan? I'll take notes as you go, so take your time."

Susan glanced at Ben and then lifted her page to read. "Frustrated, disappointed, emotional, stressed, anxious, critical, demanding, complaining, talking excessively, pushing to find a resolution and re-establish connection."

"Ben."

"I shut down, withdraw, become quiet, zone out, get flooded or overwhelmed by emotions, feel on the defensive, and create distance (both physical and emotional) in hopes of keeping the peace."

"Halfway there," I said. "The next sheet shows our underlying feelings. There's only one list for both of you to choose from."

Underlying feelings.

Vulnerable	Overwhelmed	Hopeless
Rejected	Exhausted	Panicked
Unwanted	Sad	Nervous
Abandoned	Scared	Inadequate
Dismissed	Guilty	Intimidated
Unloved	Embarrassed	Lonely
Confused	Ashamed	Unimportant

"Almost there," I said. "Two short lists to go. The first asks, *Having gone through this surge of emotions, what story are you telling yourself underneath?* And finally, the second consideration becomes, *At a time like this, what do you really need?*"

Stories I tell myself.

You don't care.

You don't really love me.

I'm in this alone.

I'll never be/do enough for you.

I won't be able to succeed.

You are going to leave.

You think I'm a failure.

You don't understand me.

I can't get anything right.

I'm not enough.

You don't appreciate me.

You think I'm a terrible person.

I don't need you/this relationship.

Life would be better on my own.

What I really need.

Love

Connection

Appreciation

Positivity

Kindness

Sweetness

Affection

To feel loved

To feel supported

To feel understood

To be seen for my best intentions

To know I am enough

To know that we are in this together

To sense you are engaged with me

To know that you want me and are happy to be with me

"Ben, you're first to share your lists."

Ben knit his eyebrows together and adjusted his glasses. "Okay, underneath I feel overwhelmed, guilty, embarrassed, hopeless, and inadequate. I tell myself that I can't ever do enough or get it right. I tell myself you think I'm a failure, and I'll never be able to make you happy. What I need is positivity, encouragement, softness, appreciation, forgiveness, kindness, sweetness, and affection—and to be seen for my best intentions."

"Susan."

"Underneath I feel alone, unimportant, exhausted, unsupported, and unloved. I tell myself that you don't care, that I'm in this alone, that you don't appreciate me, and that you don't really love me. What I need is a loving connection and to know we are in this together. I need engagement. I need to feel supported, seen, and understood."

"Let me tell you what you've just communicated," I said. "When you have a situation of conflict arise, Susan feels frustrated, disappointed, emotional, stressed, and anxious, so she becomes critical, demanding, complaining, talks excessively, and keeps pushing to find a resolution and re-establish connection." I looked up as she nodded. "When this happens, Ben feels overwhelmed, guilty, embarrassed, hopeless, and inadequate. He tells himself that he can't ever do enough or get it right. He thinks he's a failure and he'll never be able to make Susan happy. What he needs is positivity, encouragement, softness, appreciation, forgiveness, kindness, sweetness, affection, to be seen for his best intentions. He doesn't get what he needs so he shuts down, withdraws, becomes quiet, zones out, gets flooded or overwhelmed by emotions, feels on the defensive, creates distance (both physical and emotional) in hopes of keeping the peace."

Ben nodded when I looked up, so I continued. "When Susan sees him withdrawing like this, she feels alone, unimportant, exhausted, unsupported, and unloved. She tells herself that Ben doesn't care and that she's in this alone—that Ben doesn't appreciate her, and that he doesn't really love her. What she really needs is a love connection and to know both of you are in this together. She needs engagement, to feel supported, to feel seen and to feel understood. And that kicks off the cycle all over again—perhaps a little bit louder and a little bit worse."

Susan sat with her mouth open. "How did you do that? Were you recording our conversations?"

"What I want to know is how do we change all that?" Ben asked.

"That's the rest of our session," I said. "For that, you need one more handout on a new way to respond."

ATTACHMENT AND RAW SPOTS

"Your friends [partner] will know you better in the first minute you meet than your acquaintances will know you in a thousand years."[35] — Richard Bach

Gerhard and Isabella both grew up in homes with poor attachment models. Gerhard had lost his parents in an auto accident while he was young, and Isabella's mother had died of cancer when she was ten. They understood attachment was essential, but the concept was not an easy one to embrace.

Gerhard opened the door for Isabella and graciously nodded his head as she swept into the room dressed in a brilliant Brazilian blouse. "My queen," he said, "which throne would you like to sit on today?"

She batted her eyes at him and gracefully lowered herself onto the love seat. "We promise to be on our best behavior today," she said. "We know we're not victims. We're not oppressed, and we're not oppressors. We got your email about attachment and raw spots, but you'll have to explain it a bit."

I waited until Gerhard sat comfortably beside her with his arm draped around her shoulders. "It's awesome to see a couple so eager to understand their differences and learn to move forward in providing security and stability for each other."

"We know our growing up years were a mess, and we're trying to save our children from having to repeat all the pain we knew," Isabella said.

"Okay," I said. "I'll tell you what I tell others. Much of our lives, we aren't tuned into the deeper emotions of our partner. We get distracted, busy, and focused on our own thoughts and emotions. It takes special intention to hear the heart of our lover, to take risks, and to show our true selves at the core. If you can really understand what your partner needs in any particular moment and respond with an open heart—caring for them, engaging them—it will change everything."

"And what if we don't figure this attachment thing out?" Gerhard said. "Millions of people before us had never heard of such a thing, and they still survived their marriages and their families."

"Good point. The difference for us is that we are trying to thrive in our relationship and not just survive. If you feel unsafe and insecure in your relationship, your brain can trigger a sense of helplessness, and over time, that can lead to depression and anxiety."

"Welcome to my world," Isabella said. "Where were you ten years ago when I needed this?"

"The good thing is, we're not too late. You can still share your needs in a way that Gerhard can respond to. If you don't get what you need, you'll find that you start to withdraw from engagement, numb your emotions, shut down, and deny your needs. We learn to protect ourselves when no one else is there to do it. The other option is that you'll become demanding and clingy while you fight for recognition so you can get Gerhard to reassure you."

"Ah, you noticed," she said. "Did you see how he treated me on the way in? It works."

"It might work temporarily," I said, "but it won't get you to a thriving relationship. You see, you were wondering how your birth families impacted your attachment. Your family of origin is only one influence on the way you connect with others. Your natural temperament, your stress response system, your strengths, your unique needs, and the lessons you've learned from other relationships through the years also impact your relationship. Not all of this has to be bad."

Gerhard lifted his hand. "Do I understand you to be saying that a lot of things impact the way we find safety and security in this relationship, so it may be that our birth family didn't screw us up totally?"

"You're not a prisoner of your past, if that's what you're asking. You can choose, together, to move forward."

"What are these raw spots you spoke about?" Gerhard asked.

"Raw spots are those sensitive places where you feel internal pain. It's the area of life that makes us lose our emotional balance as our needs and fears take over. When we lose that place of safety with our partner, we can be overwhelmed by helplessness, shame, sadness, inadequacy, and failure. We can be consumed by fears of rejection, loss, and abandonment. We start to panic."

"Sounds familiar," Isabella said.

"Raw spots come when an attachment need is repeatedly neglected, ignored, dismissed, or abused in our relationship. There could be wounding from a past significant relationship—like a parent or lack of a parent, an uncle, a teacher, or someone we once had a romantic fling with."

"So, not having my parents, and having a harsh aunt and uncle who didn't want me, might affect me in my marriage?" Gerhard said.

"Exactly what I thought you'd say. And I'm not surprised that Isabella is impacted by her mom's early death and her having to be the mother to her siblings."

"Raw spots can also come from your own relationship," I said. "If either of you has a need and your partner is continually indifferent to you, that can, over time, become an overwhelming sense of hurt. It's impossible to be in a marriage like yours and not rub up against each other's raw spots. That's why we need to talk about them."

"Just have patience with us," Isabella said. "We're not sure what's under the surface."

"It's not me who has to be careful," I said. "I'm going to give you a list of questions and then leave the two of you to deal with the answers."

Each sheet had a list of ten questions. "Go ahead, pick any three questions, and I'll watch you two navigate what happens."

"Who do you want to go first?" Gerhard asked

"You decide. I'm just here to observe for now."

"Okay, I'll go," Isabella said. "Better to ask than to have to answer." She stood to her feet and looked down on her husband. "Do you swear to tell the truth, the whole truth, and nothing but the truth, so help you God?"

"Yikes! The inquisition," Gerhard said, holding up his arms in a mock effort to ward off an attacker. "Is this really what we're supposed to do?"

"Listen hard, buster," Isabella said. "Number one: Was there a time in your current relationship when you suddenly got thrown off balance, when something small seemed to change your sense of safety with your lover—that's me, or it better be—and instantly impacted you emotionally? The clock is ticking. Go!"

"Well, it certainly isn't now," Gerhard said. "Or maybe it is. Every once in a while, I notice you make offhanded remarks like you just did when you said, "Your lover—that's me, or it better be." I know you're teasing, but somehow it hits me and makes me feel as if I've been unfaithful somehow, or as if you think I could be. I'm thinking it could be because I know my uncle was unfaithful at least once, and I saw how deadly that was on my aunt. I think she took it out on me more because she had to hurt someone."

"Didn't see that one coming," Isabella said. "What do I do now?"

"You let Gerhard ask you another question on the sheet."

Gerhard seemed caught in a trance. "Gerhard!" I called. "If you need help, tap your hands alternately on your knees as you think of what you're seeing. Embrace yourself if it helps. You're safe here. It's okay here."

Isabella touched his shoulder and gently massaged. He shook off the memory and focused on Isabella. "Wow! This stuff is dangerous. I haven't had to think of catching my uncle with the babysitter since before we were married. When I remember my aunt screeching at that girl, it's like I hear her reminding me of how bad it is to get close to a beautiful woman."

"That's hard," Isabella said. "Do you think it would help to ask me a question?"

He nodded and picked up his sheet. "I think these all follow up on the question you already asked."

"Oh yes," I said. "I think you answered the second question. 'What was the trigger that created this sense of emotional disconnection? What did your partner specifically do or say that sparked this response?'"

"You never warned me it was going to be like this," Gerhard said. "Are you saying that hidden stuff like this can impact the way I connect with Isabella?"

"You said it yourself, Gerhard. You can still hear your aunt's voice inside, telling you not to get too close to a beautiful woman. Why do you think she was saying that? Why don't you tap your knees as you're trying to remember?"

Gerhard tapped lightly on his thighs as he focused his thoughts. "I'm pretty sure she thought pretty women would lead me astray, or cheat on me, or get me in trouble somehow."

"What was the feeling in your body in the split second before you reacted and got numb? Did you feel a tightness in your chest? An emptiness? Heat? Did you feel small, young, empty, cold, detached, or tearful?"

He stopped tapping for a moment, then resumed. "I felt young. I felt like I was in trouble again. I felt like I was seeing something I shouldn't be seeing."

"What emotions are connected to those body sensations? How did you feel in that moment?"

Gerhard furrowed his brow. "Alone... helpless... numb... afraid... terrified... ashamed... confused... disgusted... curious." He shook his head. "I don't know; it was a lot."

"That was a lot," Isabella said, rubbing his neck in gentle circles. "I'm sorry I'm so beautiful, babe. Maybe your aunt was warning you about good-looking German girls."

"I never thought of that." He smiled and patted her hand.

"Are you ready to finish the ten questions?" I asked.

He shook his head. "I think I've had enough on this raw spot for now. I'll take the sheet home and look it over. Maybe next week we can try one of Isabella's raw spots. I'm really not used to this much emotion."

ATTACHMENT AND FORGIVENESS

> **"As I walked out the door toward the gate that would lead to my freedom, I knew if I didn't leave my bitterness and hatred behind, I'd still be in prison."[36]—Nelson Mandala**

Hailey and Simon arrived a few minutes late and shrugged off their coats.

"You're forgiven," I said.

Simon glanced at Hailey. "Guess I'm needing a lot of that these days."

"Oh?"

Hailey glared sideways at Simon and then glanced back at me. "Yes, it's clear that I'm the one who is being called on to forgive over and over. I know Jesus said to forgive seventy times seven, but there has got to be a time when some serious intention is put into doing things differently."

"I guess things have gotten chaotic and run down after all these years," Simon said. "It seems that no matter how many youth we help in their troubles, there are more bringing new issues every day."

"Have you heard the parable of the fence post?" I asked. Both shook their heads, so I shared it. "Imagine a new white fence post. It sits out in the weather, year after year. What happens to it?"

"It gets old, gray—maybe cracks and falls over," Simon answered.

"Yes, if you ignore it. The same is true with your relationship. If you leave it to the elements without refreshing it, repainting it, protecting and reinforcing it, it can get old and gray."

"What's that got to do with forgiveness?" Hailey asked.

"In terms of attachment thinking, your spouse begins to feel insecure and unsafe because the need for forgiveness means your connection has been stretched. In terms of our parable, the troubled youth you serve are the elements that wear you down. Forgiveness is the refreshing, repainting, and renewing process in a relationship."

"I feel that, with some clear thinking, we could avoid a lot of the things that need forgiveness," Hailey said. "Like Friday night when Simon stayed up past midnight talking with a teen girl outside her halfway house. Or Wednesday night, when he invited a dozen guys to watch the game, then talked with them about dating until after midnight when that was our date night. We had so many complaints from parents because it was a school night. He doesn't seem to think through his choices, and I get pulled into the chaos."

"Sounds like you're talking about boundaries again. You mentioned that in our last session."

"How do we set up boundaries with so many youths in need?" Simon asked.

"You're probably already familiar with the idea that boundaries are like fences that help you avoid situations that leave you feeling pressured, manipulated, or resentful when you finish interacting with some-one.[37] They guard your attachment to each other. You are responsible for everything inside the fence and not responsible for what's outside the fence." I flipped through my binder and pulled out a handout. "You can see here that you are responsible for your own feelings. Feelings are like a mirror to let you know how your relationship is going. You're also responsible for your attitudes and beliefs. An attitude reflects your ori-entation toward someone, and beliefs are what you accept as true. None of these can be blamed on anyone else."

Boundaries.

• Feelings	• Choices	• Resources
• Attitudes	• Values	• Thoughts
• Beliefs	• Limits	• Desires
• Behaviors	• Talents	• Love

"How does this relate to forgiveness?" Simon said.

"Hailey mentioned that she thought some clear thinking could help alleviate the need for so much forgiveness. I'm showing you how to gain clear thinking by understanding boundaries. What are you responsible for, and what are you not responsible for?"

"Behaviors should fall within our boundaries," Hailey said.

"Exactly. Behaviors have consequences. We reap what we sow. Choices are also within our boundaries, and we need to avoid putting the responsibility for our choices onto others, even if they are young. To sit with a girl in your car past midnight or to stay up late with the boys on a school night is a choice. Your values are the things you assign importance to. Limits also are yours to set. How you use your talents and resources is your responsibility. How you act out your thoughts is up to you, and so is how you communicate those thoughts to others. Your desires and what you set your love on is also within your boundaries."

"So, if I'm living within my boundaries, there is a better chance I won't be having to ask for forgiveness so much?" Simon asked.

I smiled. "A better chance." I passed over another sheet of paper. "Take a look at this chart. It talks about what is in our control and what isn't."[38]

Out of My Control	In My Control
Actions of others	My thoughts
The past	My actions
Opinions of others	How I speak to myself
Circumstances around me	How I spend free time
Outcome of my efforts	How I handle challenges
The future	The goals I set
How others take care of themselves	My boundaries
What other people think of me	What I give my energy to

"You can see that all the boundaries we've been talking about are under your control. When you align your relationships within the boundaries and control areas you have, you bring security and safety to your relationship, and you establish clear understanding about when you've stepped into a place where forgiveness is warranted."

"If he only knew how to say 'I'm sorry' instead of trying to make excuses every time," Hailey said. "One clear apology where he took responsibility would break down enough barriers that I could feel close to him again. We're both counselors who help kids, but we have trouble helping ourselves stay close."

I dragged out the binder and removed a list of seven statements. "This is a guideline to help you with apologies and maybe with forgiveness as well. You two can alternate reading each one, and if you have questions, we can deal with those. The key is to put this into action."

Simon began. "One: Specifically say the words: I am sorry." He lowered the page. "I do that over and over."

"The word is *specifically*," I said. "You need to say, 'I am sorry for staying out with that girl until midnight when I know that you're at home worried; when I know it's past her curfew and she could get into trouble; and when I know this won't look good for her or me.'"

"Really?" Simon turned to Hailey. "That's what you want? You want me to grovel?"

"It's not groveling if you're specific and sincere," I said. "That is not where you finish. Hailey, read the next sentence."

She shifted an inch away from Simon and focused on her page. "Two: Express regret and remorse. Something like, 'I regret that I haven't made time for you a greater priority and that it's created a disconnection between us.'"

"We've done this for years, and you've hardly ever complained before," Simon said. "What's going on now?"

"If you can offer a sincere apology, you might find yourself connected enough to discuss all that," I said.

He lifted his paper. "Three: Offer empathy by imagining how it felt/feels for the other person. Something like 'I imagine you've been feeling lonely and sad and that you are longing for more closeness and fun.'" He pushed himself off the loveseat and paced around behind it. "How can she be lonely when we have a house full of kids? It's not like I'm the only one hanging out with them all."

"I think you're missing the point," Hailey said over her shoulder. "I'm lonely for you, for us."

He leaned against the back of the loveseat and lifted his paper. "Okay, let's see where this goes. Four: Find something to appreciate them for in this situation. That's a stretch. Something like, 'I'm grateful you want to spend time with me and for all the ways you make yourself available to me.' Now that's true. I am grateful for Hailey and all she does. I couldn't do this without her."

"Do you tell her that in your apology?"

"She knows," he said, returning to his seat. "Don't you?"

"It doesn't hurt to tell me," she responded. "Five: Take one hundred percent responsibility for your part in what occurred. Something like 'I take complete responsibility for not managing my time better and for letting work and other responsibilities get in the way of our quality time. You are my priority, and I've not been doing a good job showing you that.'"

"Wow! This is getting personal," Simon said. "Six: Ask or express how you will make it up to the other individual." He smiled. "Something like 'I really want to make it up to you. Can I take you out this Friday? Is there anything else I can do?' Are you expecting me to remember all this every time I do something wrong?"

"It might help to post this sheet somewhere and practice a few times. You'll quickly realize that thinking things out ahead of time reveals whether you're helping attachment or hurting it."

"Why don't you want to make things right with me?" Hailey asked.

"I do," Simon said. "I just didn't realize it would take this much effort."

Hailey shifted closer to her husband on the loveseat. "Seven: Ask or express how you will do it differently in the future. Don't forget, this goes both ways," she said. "I have to practice these things when I blow it too." When she saw Simon nod, she finished. "Something like 'I recommit to making our time together a priority. I've already put it on my list to delegate some of my responsibilities to the kids so this doesn't happen again. Is there anything else I can do to keep this from recurring?'"

"Seems like it's time for practicing," Simon said. "I'm committed to helping Hailey feel secure and safe in our relationship, and if this is part of what it takes, I can do this."

"Enjoy the week," I said.

ATTACHMENT AND STORIES

"The best love is the kind that awakens the soul and makes us reach for more, that plants a fire in our hearts and brings peace to our minds."[39]—Nicholas Sparks

Francis and Nyota knocked lightly and pushed the door open. My previous client was wiping her eyes, so they quickly ducked out again.

When the transition was finally made, the two of them stepped inside, arms wrapped around each other's waists. Francis had a soother in his mouth, and Nyota was dressed in ripped jeans, looking like a teenager.

"Looks like we got caught acting our emotional age again," Francis said, as he popped the soother out of his mouth. "We've been looking at that chart and trying to change our responses to each other. You said we're focusing on attachment this week, so we came attached."

The two of them moved apart, and the red bungee cord around their middle was obvious. "This is the kind of thing that brought us together," Nyota said. "We loved to laugh and do crazy things. We just drifted apart as we got busy."

"Have a seat," I said, pulling out a handout. "Do you remember the Six Pillars of a Thriving Relationship?"

"Something about sex and commitment," Francis said, grinning widely.

"Let's look at them quickly," I said.

Personal Responsibility
Secure Attachment
Repair
Communication
Positive Love Account
Physical Intimacy

"These six things will impact your attachment to each other. The stories you tell yourself about what's happening with each of the pillars will also impact your attachment—how safe and secure you feel with each other."

"What if there is no story to tell about some of those?" Francis asked. "Not that I'm looking toward the bottom of the list or anything."

Nyota raised her paper high. "I say if you want number six. you better get the other five down first."

I held my hand up as well. "I say if you want any of these, you have to get past the power struggle to the commitment that we noticed in the five stages of relationship."

I pushed another handout their way, and Nyota snatched up the paper, holding it just out of Francis's reach. When he finally snatched it—and tickled her in the process—I was sure I was losing the room.

"If we could focus just for this exercise, I'm sure you'll see something beneficial. This might help you get some direction. Francis, I want you to focus on the moment you came through the door and Nyota wasn't there. Nyota, I want you to focus on the moment you returned from seeing your friend in need. Imagine yourself clearly at that moment. What were you thinking and feeling? Take turns at each step to say what you need to say. Now, let's reconnect."

Francis cleared his throat and stood up, holding his page out at arm's length. "Step one: Commit to connection. Say this aloud to each other." He nodded. "Nyota, darling, I commit to seeing you as my ally and teammate and to learning and growing together from this day forward."

Nyota knelt on the love seat, resting the paper on the back. "Francis, honey, I commit to seeing you as my ally and teammate and to learning and growing together from this day forward."

Francis stepped closer to the love seat. "Step two: Objectively communicate the upsetting situation." He reflected for a moment. "When I walked through the door after my retreat and saw there was no note telling me where you were, I was sure something terrible must have happened to you."

Nyota sat back on her heels. "When my friend Bethany called me about needing a ride to the hospital, I dropped everything and ran. You were gone, and I thought it might be quick. She needed someone with her, and when I got that text from you, I was sure you were about as inconsiderate as anyone can get."

"This is getting pretty personal, doc," Francis said.

"Take your time. You're doing well," I said.

"Step three: Openly express your true feelings, and get into your beloved's heart." Francis took another step toward the love seat and rested a hand on Nyota's shoulder above her heart. "Glad you don't have a grinch heart," he said. "Okay, I felt confused, anxious, upset, worried, and betrayed. A bunch of stuff. And knowing what I know now, I'm sure you were feeling compassion for your friend; anxious and stressed because you weren't getting your work done; and maybe regretful that you hadn't told me where you were."

Nyota nodded. "Close. Francis, I felt overwhelmed, stressed, panicked, alone, desperate, helpless, out of control, powerless. Like you said, a bunch of stuff. I imagine you felt confused, worried, alone, tired from the retreat, relieved to be home, and glad to get a shower and change."

"Does this really work?" Francis asked. "We're saying stuff, but does it change our attachment and make Nyota feel safe and secure?"

"Let's finish, and we can talk about it."

"Step four: Articulate the story you are telling yourself. Ah, here's the rub." He rubbed the top of his head, smiling. "The story I told myself is that you don't care about me, my feelings, our promises to each other, or our covenant... that you were gone and probably not coming back again. I also told myself you might be in a car accident, or in the hospital."

"Quite the mind you have," Nyota said. "The story I told myself—after I got over my mad from that text—is that you were probably expecting me to be flouncing around in a negligee, waiting for you after your 'cranked-up-on-testosterone' retreat. You probably expected a steak dinner. I told myself you were wanting me to be your slave and wait on you hand and foot with a massage and a hot bath."

Francis raised his eyebrows. "Okay, so you know me. Step five: Take responsibility for how you reacted or got defensive." He bit his lip for a moment and then sighed. "I reacted by calling you repeatedly and leaving that text message about my frustration and worry. I actually deleted three of my messages. I was grumpy and angry when you finally walked through the door. I couldn't believe that you were so nonchalant about the whole thing."

"I reacted by deleting your text, grumbling to Bethany about what a jerk my husband was, calling up a friend to sit in with Bethany, and then pulling into a motel parking lot, thinking I might just not come home that night. I was feeling guilty, grumpy, and ready to tear your head off. That's probably enough."

Francis settled back onto the loveseat. "Step six: Uncover and express your underlying fear." He ran his fingers through his thick, wavy hair. "I reacted in this way because I was afraid of you not being as committed to our relationship as I was. I thought you might not be coming home. I thought I must have been blind to your love for me. I thought I'd been abandoned. I was also scared that something might have happened to you."

"Let's take a minute to get a drink and a breath," I said. "Coffee and tea are in the lounge, water by the bookcase."

Fifteen minutes later we sat back together again. Francis drained the last of his coffee and took a deep breath. "Step seven: Communicate your unmet needs, and guess what needs are unmet for your beloved." He took another deep breath. "I have unmet needs for appreciation, connection, understanding, communication, and security. I'm guessing you have unmet needs for autonomy, appreciation, and understanding."

"You're probably right," Nyota said. "I also have a need for a cuddle."

"Which motel was it that you wanted to check into?" Francis asked, moving his eyebrows up and down.

"As soon as we're done here, maybe I can show you," she answered, running fingers through his hair.

ATTACHMENT AND PANIC

"Weeds are flowers, too, once you get to know them."—A.A. Milne

Esther and Phil had managed one walk-and-talk during a busy week and had achieved minimal clarity on who they thought they were without labels. I could see that the sun was shining through the window, but it was not coming in through the door with the two of them. This time, however, Esther marched in and stood by the loveseat until Phil had chosen his spot. He sat on the left side, exactly like last time.

"So," Esther began, "before you ask us—as I emailed you—we only had one chance to connect. I'm feeling like Phil panics every time I confront him about something, and I'm not sure how we're going to move ahead if he's going to wilt on me."

I waited for her to find her seat. "I want you to imagine that for the past fifteen years, you have been a sheltering space for your husband. When you are emotionally available, responsive, and warm, he feels safe and secure. When you are not, he starts to feel alone and helpless."

"Isn't it the man's job to make me feel safe and secure?" Esther asked. "I'm busy working out in the real world, and I need a peaceful place to come home to."

"True, but so does Phil," I said. "You are both real people with real feelings that alert you to the level of connection you have with each other. When you feel anger, sadness, hurt, and fear, you know that something isn't working. Fear is the built-in alarm system in our amygdala to warn us that we need to be alert to a danger around us." I took the book *Created for Connection* from the shelf behind my desk. "When we're gripped by a primal panic, we become more demanding and clingier in an effort to gain some comfort or reassurance from our partner, or we withdraw and detach in order to soothe and protect ourselves," I read. [40]

"I think we both know how that works with us," Esther said. "I'm the demanding one, and Phil is the withdrawing one."

"It seems we're just not tuned into each other's needs," Phil said. "I try to get Esther's attention, but she's so distracted and caught up in her own agenda—or the agenda of others at work—that we sail past each other without connecting."

"So, you feel that you're not giving or getting clear messaging about what you need or how you care?"

"Yes," Phil said. "I just don't feel any confidence or safety in our relationship. It's easier to hole up in my computer and stop expecting Esther to respond."

"If I knew you wanted more than just sex, it might make a difference," Esther said. "I see that look in your eyes, and all I can imagine is what you've been watching on some pornography site. I'm not an object to satisfy your lusts and desires."

"It sounds like you're feeling the strain of disconnection," I said. "You're sensing the erosion of connection and trust. You're feeling the pain and despair of feeling stuck. You're in a dance that just won't end." Phil nodded, so I continued. "The thing to realize is that you're both looking for deep attachment, and you just haven't figured out how to get what you want. You get into your 'pursue and withdraw pattern,' and that spills into other parts of life. As a result, you don't talk, and you don't experience intimacy. You end up feeling the resentment and distance."

"Are you saying that our real problem is that we're starving emotionally because we're not connecting with each other?" Esther asked. "The last counselor told me I needed to work on my communication skills, sort out my childhood trauma, and push through our differences."

I returned to the book I'd been holding. "Let me read you a quote," I said. 'The demise of marriages begins with a growing absence of responsive, intimate interactions. The conflict comes later.'"[41]

"Okay, I get all this," Esther said. "How do we get past this dance?"

I pulled a handout from my binder. "There's a cycle that starts when someone triggers your core fear. Take a look at this sheet. Identify what you are really afraid of. Esther, why don't you read this list?"

• Rejected	• Abandoned
• Disconnected	• A Failure
• Helpless	• Defective
• Inadequate	• Inferior
• Invalidated	• Unloved
• Dissatisfied	• Cheated
• Worthless	• Unaccepted
• Judged	• Humiliated
• Ignored	• Insignificant[42]

"What if we have more than one fear?" Esther asked. "I'm afraid of being rejected, defective, inadequate, unaccepted, insignificant, and maybe judged."

"That's normal," I said.

"That's a lot of fear," Phil said. "I would never have imagined all that of you."

"What are your fears?" I asked Phil.

"I have several fears, as well," Phil said, "but my core fears are being abandoned, feeling like a failure, and feeling inferior, unloved, and insignificant."

"Okay, let's go with one of your fears," I suggested. "What's your usual reaction from the following list? Phil, you read the options this time."

Phil took the sheet and focused.

• Withdrawal	• Escalation
• Try harder	• Negative beliefs
• Blaming	• Exaggeration
• Tantrums	• Denial
• Invalidation	• Defensiveness
• Clinginess	• Passive-aggressive
• Caretaking	• Acting out
• Fix-it mode	• Complaining
• Aggression or abuse	• Manipulation
• Anger and rage	• Catastrophizing
• Numbing out	• Humor
• Sarcasm	• Minimization
• Rationalization	• Indifference
• Abdication	• Self-abandonment
• Sadness	

"A lot of options on this for sure," Phil said. "If I feel my core fear is abandonment, I guess I would react with clinginess, withdrawal or numbing out."

Esther took the sheet and furrowed her brows. "I'd say if my core fear is being rejected, then I'd react by trying harder, blaming, getting defensive, and maybe getting angry."

"Phil, take a look at the third list. More feelings. This is how you feel after your partner reacts."

- Unsure
- Puzzled
- Sullen
- Hurt
- Wearied
- Shamed
- Confused
- Disgusted
- Bitter
- Frustrated
- Guilty
- Frightened
- Horrified
- Furious

- Apathetic
- Upset
- Sad
- Disappointed
- Torn up
- Uncomfortable
- Worried
- Resentful
- Fed up
- Miserable
- Embarrassed
- Anxious
- Disturbed

"Last list," I said, handing the sheet to Esther. "This is what you really want but aren't getting."

- Acceptance
- Connection
- Success
- Understanding
- Validation
- Respect
- Honor
- Commitment
- Attention
- Approval

- Grace
- Companionship
- Self-determination
- Love
- Competence
- Worth
- Dignity
- Significance
- Support
- Wanted

- Safety
- Trust
- Joy

- Affection
- Hope

"Take a look at what you really want from each other," I said, fashioning a circle on a piece of paper. "Draw a circle and put *want* in the middle of the circle. Set up four quadrants on the outside of the circle. Think of a specific situation where your core need was threatened. What fear did it bring about? List that core fear in the first quadrant. In the second quadrant, write the way you reacted. In the third quadrant, list your partner's core fear. In the fourth quadrant, record the way your partner reacted." I finished drawing out the circle and quadrants. "So, here is the dance. I hurt because I don't get what I want, so I fear and then react. This creates hurt for you because you don't get what you want, so you fear and then react, which hurts me again. And so on."

"You're saying that it's hard to feel safe and secure with each other when this kind of emotion and reaction is happening all the time," Esther said.

"I think you got it," I said. "Why don't you spend time this week tracking some of your circles, and see what you can do differently? The goal is for you to feel safe and secure again."

"Before we go, could you give us one more thing to help me deal with all this emotion?" Esther asked.

"Have you heard of the *magic and*?[43] It's something to use when you're feeling an overwhelming emotion. The idea is that what we focus on is what we feel. The *magic and* will allow you to honor your feelings but will also create an empowering life story that can help your well-being. We adopt a learning orientation toward life, so every experience can become beneficial. It's like Joseph saying to his brothers, *"You intended to harm me, but God intended it for good to accomplish what is now being done, the saving of many lives"* (Genesis 50:20). Through growth, we turn a minus into a plus. In doing that, you change your whole perspective on a situation."

"Okay, how do I do that, specifically?" Esther asked.

"Step one: Name the challenge you are currently experiencing. Freely express your thoughts and feelings. Step two: Add the *magic and* by answering these questions:

- How could it have been worse?
- What do you also appreciate about the situation?
- What can you gain from this challenge?
- How can you use it to help you grow?
- If you were to see the other individuals involved as your teachers right now, what are they here to help you learn?
- How is this happening for you, rather than simply to you?
- What is the gift in this?
- How did it help you prepare for a future experience/challenge?
- How can you better serve others because of this?

"Looks like we have some work to do," Phil said.

QUAGMIRE THREE

Calling

**"As soon as I saw you, I knew an
adventure was going to happen."
—Winnie the Pooh**

WHY DO YOU DO WHAT YOU DO?

In your imagination, picture a pair of horses pulling a carriage. Ministry is the carriage, and you and your spouse are the horses. If you pull together toward a common destination, the track of the carriage behind you will give evidence of that.

Calling is the great *why*. For followers of Jesus, that would include the Great Commission, but how does this dovetail with the great covenant we make as partners in ministry?

Many couples assume that if they've responded to their calling, a sense of *shalom* will surround them. *Shalom* is the Hebrew word which carries the meaning of peace, harmony, completeness, prosperity, wholeness, health, positive welfare, and tranquility. Not too many think that their calling may include struggle, refining, and pruning.

Ministry and marriage can come into conflict around the issue of calling when we see our calling as a target different than our spouse's. It can create tension when there are differences in theology, convictions, gifts and strengths, schedules, and patterns of communication. Another source of tension can be stress with our authorities. Sometimes our feelings to overexposure or underexposure to significant relationships in ministry, and to time with each other, can affect our mental, physical, and spiritual settledness with our ministry.

You may also feel like your conflict is greater than your calling if you don't match well on the five fundamental personality dimensions. This would mean that you have serious opposition on the extraversion-introversion scale; the agreeable-disagreeable scale; the conscientiousness-unconscientiousness scale; the orderly-disorderly scale; and the trust-mistrust scale.

CALLING AS A TARGET

"It never hurts to keep looking for sunshine."
—Winnie the Pooh

Esther and Phil arrived via Zoom and prepared to focus on how their sense of calling had twisted them into their current quagmire. I adjusted the screen for better lighting and settled in with a mug of hot water and honey.

Esther set the table for the discussion. She raised a piece of paper, and I nodded toward her. She read confidently, "Brené Brown says, 'Fitting in and belonging are not the same thing. In fact, fitting in is one of the greatest barriers to belonging. Fitting in is about assessing a situation and becoming who you need to be in order to be accepted. Belonging, on the other hand, doesn't require us to change who we are; it requires us to be who we are.'[44] I'm just being who I was made to be. I don't see the problem."

Phil leaned forward toward the screen. "I just don't appreciate the sense of superiority that comes with Esther thinking that her work in ministry is more important than what I do."

"It sounds like you've been around the block on this a few times," I said. "It sounds like you're in a hard space. If I say something that misses the mark, let me know. This is a great issue to work through so we can realize we're on the same team and moving in the same direction."

"That's all I'm looking for," Phil said.

"Don't make me out to be the bad guy here," Esther said. "We agreed that this is the way we were going to use our gifts and talents. I can't help it if my work is more demanding."

I held up my hand. "I know things are tense at home, but while we're together, we are going to try to find our way forward in a positive way. Do you think you can walk with me on this?"

They both nodded, so I continued.

"There is a sense in which work is built into the essence of what it means to be human.[45] We were created with a passion for meaningful effort and production. Our first parents are shown to be workers and stewards in a garden. God himself is seen as working. Can you agree with this?"

They both nodded.

"All work done on his behalf must be valued and seen as significant. Our society tends to monetize productivity done for social benefit, but most ministry leaders realize that much valuable work is unpaid and unrewarded in any tangible way. The same effort may be work for one and leisure for another."

"No argument from me," Phil said.

"Nor from me," Esther said. "We couldn't function without committed volunteers."

I continued. "For those who grow up in Christian ministry circles, the concept of calling may be familiar. There is a general consensus that God does lead people to specific types of vocations, jobs, and work. While all work is sacred to followers of Jesus, there is an idea for a few that some work is considered spiritual and some secular."

"The issue is where you draw the line," Phil interjected. "Much of my work helps non-profits. I think it's about the one doing the work rather than the work itself that makes it spiritual."

I looked toward Esther, and she shrugged. "Nothing more to say on that. He somehow feels like I'm undermining his manhood just because I have to keep some things confidential in the church."

"This is not about my manhood," Phil said. "It's about our calling."

"Let's focus on that," I said. "The call to every believer is first to follow Jesus, and it's the acceptance of this call that supersedes all other calls to specific ministry or vocation. Both husband and wife are called to follow Jesus in making disciples, and this is the point of unity that all other callings must be anchored to."[46]

"What is the value of having a call if it's the same for everyone?" Esther asked.

"A calling helps you transcend fear, discouragement, doubt, shame, guilt, and pain," I said. "It unleashes strength, courage, hope, truth, healing, and peace when you can't find those things on your own."

Phil signalled for attention by flashing a raised hand on his screen. "What happens when the identity of one member of the couple collides with the calling that is felt by the other partner?"

"It used to be that covenant and calling were one and the same for a couple. Many wedding ceremonies included the words of Ruth where the woman said to her future husband, *'Where you go I will go, and where you stay I will stay. Your people will be my people and your God my God. Where you die I will die, and there I will be buried'* (Ruth 1:16,17). This may no longer be so automatic."

"Automatic!" Esther chimed in. "Maybe for my grandmother. I've never heard anyone our age still say all that."

"Okay," I acknowledged. "I wasn't done. How do we find our way forward from here?"

Phil's face filled the screen as he leaned toward the camera. "I want to admit that the way I was raised impacted my thinking. I grew up thinking I didn't have much choice in my world, and I still react when I feel my choice is being taken away."

"Are you saying that the authorities in your world didn't give you a sense of freedom to make choices, and that you still feel like that helpless child when your options are removed?"

"That's exactly what he's saying," Esther said. "He feels controlled, and that hits him deep."

"I know that my parents, teachers, and coaches wanted to keep me safe," Phil said, "but it left me feeling like I was always doing the wrong thing."

"So how did God's calling fit into all that?" I asked.

"I grew up thinking God's will was like a bullseye I had to hit," Phil replied. "He made all the choices for me before I was born, and I had to find the right mate, the right work, the right place to live. Anytime I thought I'd found what God wanted for me, I fixated on that, and didn't feel I could move on."

"So, God's calling feels like a target you have to hit," I said. "Something where you have no choice. When things start feeling out of control, you try to control the one you love so they don't miss out on what God wants."

"Sort of," Phil said.

"Can you see how viewing your calling as a target can set you up for conflict when your spouse is aiming at a different target?"

"I can see why we need regular check-ins to make sure we're going in the same direction," Esther said. "At work, we have daily, weekly, monthly, and quarterly check-ins with the team. Maybe we ought to schedule something similar at home."

CALLING AND THEOLOGY

"It makes such a difference to have someone who believes in you." —Winnie the Pooh

Ben and Susan transitioned into this quagmire of calling during their fourth session. When I walked into my office, they were already standing at the window. They took one more glance at the city skyline, then headed right for the loveseat. Susan wanted to show me pictures of a family outing, but Ben wanted to focus on the theology he'd been pondering. His loud sigh let us know we'd seen enough images of the kids.

"We need to settle this issue of calling," he said. "We're on two different pages when it comes to understanding what it means for us as a couple. Where do we start?"

I helped set the table for the discussion. "Calling is a charged concept for many followers of Jesus. Some think of calling as a dramatic experience. For example, Noah building an ark, Abraham leaving home to establish a new nation, Jonah being called to Nineveh to preach repentance, or Saul going to preach to the Gentiles. Some see it as a personal calling to follow Jesus in the same way Matthew, Peter, and John were summoned."

Ben was ready with a quote he had copied out. "Os Guiness says, 'Calling is the truth that God calls us to himself so decisively that everything we are, everything we do, and everything we have is invested with a special devotion, dynamism, and direction lived out as a response to his summons and service.' He says that calling gets your attention, establishes you with a purpose, sets you apart through relationship, and unleashes you for tasks like peace, fellowship, eternal life, suffering, discipleship, and service. He sees calling as a 'metaphor for the life of faith itself.' He says we are primarily called to someone, and not to something, or somewhere. Secondarily, 'everyone, everywhere, and in everything, should think, speak, live and act entirely for him' and this can be in the home, the neighborhood, or the workplace. He sees conflict as happening when these two types of calling get out of order."[47]

"Os Guiness is a wise man," I said. "Are you agreeing that you have the two aspects of calling out of order in your relationship with Susan? How does your covenant fit into your understanding of calling? Does your wife have the same first calling as you but a different second calling?"

"I try to keep the two distinct," Ben said. "How are you bringing them together?"

"Let me try by saying this," I said. "Once the historical church is established at Pentecost, some see calling more in line with gifting, in that individuals discern where in the body of Christ they are meant to serve. This involves examining character, abilities, needs, passions, experience, and roles. In this sense, everyone is called to contribute to the furtherance of God's kingdom."

"How does that apply to our marriage?" Ben asked.

"I don't like people calling me the pastor's wife," Susan blurted out. "It's as if I don't have my own calling to make disciples, as if I'm some unpaid appendage, a bonus that lets the church get a two-for-one deal." She glanced quickly at Ben. "I don't want to go to the church feeling all those expectations, as if I'm going to fill in all the gaps my husband leaves."

"Many tests have been developed to help bring some objectivity and support to a couple's search for understanding in this area,"[48] I said.

"How did you and your wife handle your calling?" Susan asked.

"Calling can easily become a quagmire," I answered. "For example, at my graduation ceremony, after four years in theological college, one of my mentoring profs declared that I must become a preacher. I began to explore that option. My wife, Gayle, informed me with no uncertainty that she was not going to be a pastor's wife, so forget it. I was a bit relieved and went on to take my teaching credentials. To be fair, we both felt a call toward missions, and my training was meant to be in preparation for that call."

"So, you gave in to your wife?" Ben said. "What about your call?"

I held up both hands as if stopping a ball thrown in my direction. "My wife is an incredible woman of prayer, and I trust her discernment, so it was surprising when some time later, she told me that God had worked with her to suggest I go back to seminary and become a pastor. There are several things we consider when we listen for direction. What is Scripture saying to us independently and together? What are circumstances—and the needs around—showing us? What promptings are happening as we pray, listen to messages, consider our gifting, and chat with friends? What are the wise counselors in our life saying? What God-things are we seeing at work? Some feel an internal tugging or passion growing. When these start to align in a clear direction, we discern for next steps. It's when these things don't align for a ministry couple that conflicts can occur."

"So, you think we haven't paid attention along the way to all the signs God set out?" Ben asked.

"I'm merely answering Susan on how my wife and I dealt with our sense of calling. You may want to examine the story you have created to summarize your sense of call. Perhaps one of you had a Damascus Road encounter with Jesus, where the call is clear and convicting. Or perhaps you've felt a call like Jeremiah, from an early age. This may not be the usual experience in most circles compared to the gradual, progressive sense of call that grows over time, experience, and community discernment. Your involvement in a ministry or service opportunity may open the door to a call you hadn't considered."

"Like changing diapers?" Susan asked.

"It's not the details but the story of what you're telling yourself about why you do what you do. It's also the process of how you got here. Talk through the things you've come to believe together; talk about why you're here."

"So, that's all there is to it?" Ben asked.

"It's also the respect you bring to each other. You may remember reading about Martin Buber's perspective on relationships. When we approach our spouse as if they're a part of us, we begin to treat them as objects to accomplish something we have in our own minds. We dump our work on them without proper greeting; we talk down about others who do it differently than us; we treat others as if they don't have their own 'freedom, dreams, autonomy.'"[49]

"And you think that's what I'm doing with Susan?"

"Only you know what you're thinking about her when you leave her to run the nursery, take care of things at home, manage the finances, and do the shopping with children in tow. All I'm saying is that your spouse will feel the level of respect you give to their calling by the way you treat them. You'll move from defensiveness and reactivity to openness and vulnerability."

"I guess we have some talking to do," Ben said.

"Talking is a first step," I said. "When there is false peace in the house, there will never be true partnership in your calling. Conflicts will remain unresolved, truth will be ignored, pain will fester and reap its consequences. You can't build something lasting on deception and pretense. Yes, you need to do the wise and loving thing, but don't make every decision a life-and-death issue."

"So, how would you summarize the difference between our calling, our covenant, and our commission?" Ben persisted.

"Let me ask you something," I said. "Do you see conflict between the Great Commission and the great covenant?"

Ben ran his fingers through his hair and grimaced. "The first thing gets me out of the house, and the second one keeps me at home. That can create conflict."

"I'm talking the theology of the two. Part of the issue is that you have embraced the concept that making disciples means individually recruiting people to assent to a list of affirmed statements and prescribed activities. Your faith is an intellectual and physical act without embracing the spiritual and emotional. This draws boundaries between yourself and others. How did Jesus summarize everything in his new commandment?"

Ben leaned forward. "To love one another as he loved us."

"Yes! The apostle Paul calls this the way of love and tells us to walk, or live, in it.[50] Making disciples means a community-focused embracing of demonstrated sacrificial and humble service in the agape relationships at home and in the world around us. This is your calling, and it brings the Great Commission and the great covenant together as one. Too often, we recruit people to renew their minds without renewing their hearts."

"So, you think I'm making this all too complicated?"

"Think of the difference between practicing God's grace from your heart and from your mind. Which one opens others up to the Spirit's conviction and transformation? Which one draws people together? Which one would your wife appreciate?"

"You have a point," Ben said. "If our calling is to love, that would simplify a lot."

"Count me in," Susan said. "I don't think it should take a seminary degree to live like we're supposed to."

CALLING AND CONVICTIONS

"I'm not lost, for I know where I am. But however, where I am may be lost." —Winnie the Pooh

Jim and Sharon followed their typical routine of looking over the skyline before settling into the loveseat. The air was cooler today, and their thicker sweaters were dumped casually onto the chairs by my desk. Jim checked his watch, then glanced at the digital clock I had perched on a wall space near the door. We caught up on their week in a few moments. They had focused their devotional readings on several British authors and had discussed the impact of these insights on their partnership in ministry. Jim had written down some quotes on pieces of lined paper and shared one reading while Sharon read another.

Jim laid the paper on his lap. "British pastor Charles H. Spurgeon said to those considering pastoral ministry, 'If you can do anything else, do it. If you can stay out of the ministry, stay out of the ministry.'[51] What do you think about that now that we're neck deep in it?"

"It's really not that important what I think," I replied. "It's what the two of you have come to believe and how it affects your relationship. I would add that if your spouse is adamantly opposed to the ministry you feel called to, that's a sign to consider doing something else. Trying to convict, coerce, convince, or compel your spouse to follow your lead against their desires is a sure path to collision—and even the dismantling of your covenant."

"Part of our problem is that we don't feel together on this," Sharon said. "Jim told me that he'd been reading Jeremiah 1:5 and that God had impressed on him the call."

I flipped open my Bible. "Let me read that passage aloud, and see what you think," I said. "'*The word of the Lord came to me, saying, "Before I formed you in the womb I knew you, before you were born, I set you apart; I appointed you as a prophet to the nations."*' Now, was that written specifically to you, Jim?"

Jim sank back into the loveseat as Sharon leaned forward.

"Of course we have to be careful with our interpretation of Scripture. Do you think we should back out if we both don't feel the same way?" Sharon asked.

"Let me add something to the wisdom from Charles Spurgeon," I said. "Lloyd-Jones believed there were six things a minister would possess if they're called to the pulpit. These include an inner compulsion and holy preoccupation they can't ignore; a confirmation and affirmation from wise outside leaders who see God's hand on their life; an overwhelming compassion for the people of God and the lost; a powerful constraint to do this work no matter what; sobriety over one's inability to do the task and the humility to press forward; and a formal commissioning by leaders who recognize the candidate's gifting and character."[52]

"Is that only for ministers who are called to the pulpit?" Jim asked. "What about for other callings?"

"You likely wouldn't have the same qualities for a calling outside the pulpit. You can see that these six evidences would make it hard for one to turn away from the path ahead. Unfortunately, for Lloyd-Jones, there is no mention of the aligned agreement with one's spouse— that they would also bear the weight of this shared calling. Marriage is equally a calling—along with leisure, work, and worship. The issues are balance and relationship. Sometimes, circumstances prevent us from having the desires of our heart, and we must do what is before us to meet the needs of our family."

"So, you think ministry is a higher and holier calling than other things?" Sharon asked.

"I didn't say that, but I don't have to live with your choice or calling. Some see God calling Noah to build an ark, Moses and Aaron to build a tabernacle, and Solomon to build a temple—and they discern that this is what a calling looks like. This kind of specific direction to a specific task may not be as common in our day and age. It may be that God expects us to notice the needs in our family, community, and world, and then put our efforts into alleviating these needs as we are able.[53] The key is communication so that both partners move in the same direction."

"I think we've figured out how to get around most marriage hurdles," Jim said. "This work thing sometimes gets in the way. Being together is our favorite place. We just need to figure out how to do it better."

"Work is about serving the common good, but it cannot be elevated to the position of an idol where we look to it to meet our core needs. It cannot take the place of God, our spouse, or our place of worship in satisfying our desires. There are many thoughtful resources available if this issue becomes a source of contention for either spouse."[54]

"It's crazy when the smallest things can set us off, and it usually is work related," Jim said. "We get saying things, and it's like hitting each other with poison darts."

"When we bring God into why we do what we do, then collision is just around the corner. Yet we can't not do that. God's will and calling become like a trump card in our debate. The poisons that spew off our tongue get sanctified, and we gain a holy boldness which crushes the one we love." I opened my binder and pulled out a few handouts. "Calling can be a cover to manipulate for a love and relationship we sense we're not getting. We need to take radical responsibility for what we do without blaming another. When we take responsibility for our own actions, it frees our partner from having to point things out and lessens the temperature in the relationship."

"I see you've dealt with this before," Sharon said, reaching for the handout.

"Relationship poisons are really strategies we use to get our hidden needs met. They can be used to confirm our sense of call when we feel threatened. Mostly, they are really a cry for connection when we feel it's being stretched. Our sense of calling and covenant might be in conflict."

"This sheet looks like a lot of poison," Jim said. "How does this work?"

"Based on the modeling of our birth families, the examples of families we know, or our own experience in marriage, we will attempt different strategies to reach out to someone we hope can connect with us at a heart level. There are ten unhealthy strategies we might use. Why don't you use a yellow highlighter to see which ones you've utilized in your relationship, and consider how these may be increasing the conflict between ministry and marriage?"

Blame and criticism might include punishing or looking down on your partner; pointing out everything your partner does wrong; criticism; staying in a victim role; or shaming your partner and trying to make them feel badly.

Contempt might show up through name calling; looking down on your partner; ridicule and teasing; expressing a mix of disgust and anger; eye rolling; or mimicking your partner.

Controlling and dominating might show up through talking excessively or loudly to speak over your partner; manipulating; nagging; physical aggression or violence; psychoanalyzing your partner; coercing or pressuring your partner to do something they don't want to do; gaslighting; or valuing your ideas as more valid than your partner's because of your background.

Checking out (physically, mentally, or emotionally) might show up by giving the silent treatment; stonewalling (refusing to communicate or cooperate); withdrawing; shutting down; using tiredness as an excuse to check out; or going to friends or family to complain rather than to your beloved to find solutions.

Defensiveness may be shown through thinking you know it all; having to be right; being unwilling to change; assuming closed body posture when your partner speaks; defensiveness; arguing or problem solving when highly triggered; invalidating other person's feelings or thoughts; or resistance or unwillingness to take responsibility or give an apology.

Resentment may involve using the past as a weapon; unwillingness to forgive; or continually reminding your beloved of their past mistakes, despite their positive changes.

Secrets and dishonesty can include being in denial; not being honest with yourself; pretending everything is okay; secrets; affairs (emotional and / or physical); holding feelings in; hiding; creating drama to get attention; giving in when you don't mean it; or threatening to leave, even when you don't mean it.

Believing everything you think through the stories you tell yourself. This might show up when you take things personally; overthink; project (accuse your partner of something you do); exaggerate problems to yourself; or idealize past relationships.

Neglecting the relationship can be evident when you don't make your partner a priority; when there is a lack of affection; when you determine to take care of yourself and you do; when you keep score of who does more; when you ignore your partner; or when you don't follow through.

Not loving and caring for yourself can be seen through neglecting self-care; addictions or other destructive behaviors; not managing stress and anxiety; getting clingy (not giving your partner space); not tending to your health; isolating from people outside your relationship; expecting your partner to meet all your needs; jealousy; self-judgment; unresolved wounds from the past; or becoming overly passive so you lose yourself and your voice.[55]

"Taking personal responsibility for how you impact your relationship is essential. For this exercise, I want you to take turns reading off the phrases you have highlighted. Start by saying, "In the area of blame and criticism, I show this to you by... " and then list what you do, one thing at a time—alternating back and forth—until you get to the next category. Don't comment on what your partner says. Just focus on what you do. When we're done, we'll see what we can do about all this."

CALLING AND STRENGTHS

> **"A good marriage is one which allows for change and growth in the individuals and in the way they express their love."[56] — Pearl S. Buck**

Sam and Hannah still sat in separate chairs as I brought up the issue of calling. Hannah had been mulling over their personality tests from the second session, and we needed to discuss that more before moving on.

She held up the paperwork. "So, I'm still not settled about how our personalities could possibly work together. If Sam is an ENFJ (Teacher) and I'm an ISTJ (Inspector), we are opposites. He looks like some kind of hero. He embraces emotional experience, empathizes with others, and creates harmony. Then look at me. I'm supposed to be quiet, careful, and love stability and order." She raised the papers, released them, and let them flutter to the ground. "That's the kind of order and stability I've brought. He drives me crazy. He knows I need structure and organization; he knows I need things to be logical, and that I'm skeptical about emotion. I'm focused on my current experience, and I don't live in the world of abstract ideas. I can't live with a man who has his head in the clouds, getting all emotional even when we watch a movie."

Sam slumped in place. "I just want to show you that I love you."

"See! You make me out to be a heartless witch. I feel manipulated by your emotions, as if I must give up what I feel called to do in order to let you do whatever you want to do."

I intervened. "Okay, remember now. Respect is our bottom line. Both of you need to give each other the space to feel comfortable in your world of ideas or tasks. Refraining from poisonous comments that spiral your conversations downward is essential. Valuing and honoring your partner's way of living in the world is foundational if things are to be stable. You may have to develop some outside friendships to confide in. Or you could journal. But it would be most helpful if you went for a walk and remembered some of the good times you've shared so far. By creating a bucket list, you can establish a history of shared experience to fall back on when things get tense."

"So, where do we go from here?" Sam asked.

"Do you remember when you first fell in love?" I asked. "How you noticed the best qualities about each other? As your relationship grew, you saw more and more of the whole person you had embraced. Maybe you got disenchanted and resentful, but you'd already made a public commitment. You started seeing the worst in your partner and forgot about the strengths of your best friend."

Sam nodded. "Yes, guilty. When we fell in love, I saw Hannah as organized, successful, and on top of everything. Once we'd been married a few years, and things got overwhelming in ministry, I felt as if I wore this intense straightjacket—as if she was controlling everything."

Hannah leaned forward. "Yeah, I guess I fell in love with your carefree and charismatic personality, which seemed larger than life. It seemed so freeing before we had kids. Then, I felt like you were irresponsible, overbearing, and inconsiderate. Maybe that's still part of my problem. I feel you turn the world I'm trying to organize into chaos, and I can't keep up with it all."

"Okay," I said. "We're turning a corner. When you focus on each other's positive strengths, it helps encourage those traits. You might think that God has put you in a position to point out all your partner's growth areas, but that isn't necessary. If you've tried this, you'll realize how much it impacts your intimacy, happiness, and peace."

"Yes, I have enough stuff going on in my own head without anything from the outside," Sam said. "And I'll admit, Hannah didn't hire me to be her inner critic. She probably needs some celebration and acknowledgement."

I gave them another handout. "Here's your chance to follow through. On this paper, there are about a hundred listed. I want you to read through the list and circle the top ten-to-fifteen strengths you see in your partner. We'll talk about the top five, and you can share a story on how your spouse has lived out that trait. If you can think of any other positive strengths, add them to the list below:"

Strengths

Adaptable, Accommodating, Adventuresome, Analytical, Articulate, Attractive, Authentic,

Beautiful, Believable, Benevolent, Bold, Brainy, Brave, Builder, Bustling, Busy,

Calm, Careful, Caring, Cheerful, Comforting, Communicative, Compassionate, Complex, Confident, Conscientious, Cooperative, Courageous, Creative, Curious,

Decisive, Dependable, Determined, Diplomatic, Disciplined, Discreet, Dynamic,

Effervescent, Empathic, Empowered, Encouraging, Engaged, Enthusiastic, Experimental,

Fair, Faithful, Fervent, Flexible, Firm, Flourishing, Free-spirited, Friendly, Fun, Funny,

Gainful, Generous, Gentle, Genuine, Graceful, Grateful, Great Memory, Guardian,

Happy, Harmonious, Healthy, High energy, Honest, Hopeful, Humble, Humorous,

Imaginative, Independent, Industrious, Innovative, Insightful, Inspiring, Integrity, Intelligent,

Jolly, Jovial, Joyful, Judicious, Just, Kind, Kindred-spirit, Knowable, Knowledgeable,

Laudable, Learned, Leader, Learns quickly, Lighthearted, Loves learning, Loving, Loyal,

Magical, Magnetic, Majestic, Memorable, Mannerly, Mature, Mechanical, Methodical, Mindful, Mobilizing, Motivator, Musical,

Nonjudgmental, Nurturing, Observant, Open-minded, Optimistic, Orderly, Organized,

Passionate, Peaceful, Persevering, Persistent, Playful, Positive, Proactive, Proud, Prudent,

Quick thinker, Quiet, Ready, Realist, Reassuring, Reflective, Resourceful, Risk-taking,

Safe, Self-aware, Self-starter, Sensitive to others, Service-oriented, Silly, Simple, Social, Socially responsible, Spiritual, Spontaneous, Supportive,

Tasteful, Team-oriented, Tenacious, Tender, Tolerant, Trusting, Trustworthy,

Understandable, Understanding, Visionary, Vivacious, Well-spoken, Willing, Wise

Other:[57]

"When we're done, take the list home and, every day, try to find one of these strengths that you can sincerely compliment your partner on. Be specific. For example, 'I thought that was really wise when you told the politician on the phone that you were carefully thinking through your choices.' Or 'Hon, I appreciated how diplomatic you were in the way you handled our kids when they were fighting over their chores.' Or

'Love, I am so thankful for how supportive you've been in understanding all the stress I've recently had at work.'"

"So, what do these strengths have to do with our calling?" Hannah asked.

"Have you considered that when God called you into a covenant relationship, that the strengths the two of you have together may have been part of his guidance on your vocational calling?"

"Wait a minute," Hannah said. "They hired him, not me. I have nothing to do with his ministry."

"And perhaps that is part of why you are having a conflict. You feel like you have nothing to do with what you see as his calling. What would happen if you both got together, recorded your strengths, and prayed about how God might call both of you? Not into a profession but into a ministry you might both feel a part of. It might not be what either of you are being paid to do, but it should be something you both know you're a part of."

"So, you're saying God gave us our strengths for a reason?" Sam asked.

"If the Psalmist thinks God fashioned you together in the womb— and if he created you to do good works, which he prepared in advance for you to do[58]—then maybe you have your strengths for a reason. If you focus on the worst, it will bring out the worst; but if you can focus on the best, it just may bring out the best."

"Makes sense to me," Hannah said.

CALLING AND SCHEDULE

> **"One of the advantages of being disorganized is that one is always having surprising discoveries." —**
> **Winnie the Pooh**

Francis and Nyota arrived smiling and plopped down on the loveseat. "You're going to be out of business soon," Francis said. "There's a certain motel that is doing the job for us. I'm desperately trying to put all the notes from my convention into practice, but Nyota can't wait that long."

"We've figured out our calling and our covenant so far," Nyota said. "The issue for us is how to find balance in our life, and to align it with our calling."

"Let's get down to work. We're going to rate each area of your life to see what is good and what needs to grow a little more. On the paper I just gave you, you'll notice the large circle with eight different segments dividing it like a pie. Inside the larger circle, you'll see ten concentric circles labeled one through ten. Francis, will you please read the headings for each section of the pie?"

Francis took one page and handed a duplicate copy to Nyota.

Wheel of balance.
- Friends and family
- Living environment
- Spirituality and personal growth
- Career and purpose
- Health and fitness
- Fun and recreation
- Romantic relationship

"Can you divide some of those pie shapes into two?" Nyota asked. "My friends and family are definitely rated differently. My career and purpose might also be split."

I slid two yellow highlighters and then two orange ones across the desk. "The first thing to do is rate how you're doing in each area. The inner circle with the small number one in it indicates you are not doing well at all. The ten, at the outer rim, says you couldn't be doing better in that area. Draw a line around the shape so you can clearly see the level. For example, if you are at a five for family, then draw a line within the pie shape at the five-circle mark, then shade it in with either yellow or orange. Do that for each section. Let's do the first one together. Nyota, what level would you say you're at with your health and fitness?"

"Ouch! You would start with that one," she said. "On a good day, I'm maybe doing like a five."

"I'm at a seven," Francis said. "One for the good guys."

"This isn't a competition," I said. "You're a team, and you're meant to be helping each other get toward ten. We'll talk about that later. Let's look at Finances."

"I'm at a seven," Nyota said. "It's hard to have enough of those green backs."

"I'm probably at a six," Francis said. "There's a lot going out of my pocket to help all the charitable causes, and the needs are way bigger than I can impact."

"Okay, finish off the rest of the wheel and then we'll look at the shape of your life," I said. "Again, feel free to split sections in two if you need to."

The two of them spent ten minutes drawing out their pie chart. Nyota was the first to hold up her warped diagram. "Looks like a tire that's been chopped up and discarded in the trash heap."

Francis set his diagram down beside hers. It also looked like a disaster of a wheel. "Looks like we have a lot of work to do," he said.

"So, let's look at the categories that are lowest, and brainstorm how we can move them toward a ten."

"What does all this have to do with calling?" Francis said. "All I see is that our life is out of balance."

"What you're seeing is how to keep your calling effective and energized," I said. "If your relationships are struggling, your finances are out of order, and your health is lagging—like I see on your wheel—then your calling isn't going to be realized the way you'd hope."

"You're asking us, for each of these areas, what it would take to bring them to a ten," Nyota said. "If we start with finances, I think it would help if we were both involved in setting the budget each year. We're involved with so many causes and people that it's hard to manage our income. Of course, we tithe and pay off our bills, but there never seems to be enough at the end of the month, and I'm concerned about our debt."

"Setting up a coordinated budget and managing monthly expenses is a good start," I said. "Is that enough to bring it to a ten?"

"I'd like to set up a discretionary generosity fund where we can use a set amount of cash to give out as we see a need in our area of ministry,"

Francis said. "I feel like I'm having to take money out of an area designated for future expenses in order to cover an immediate emergency."

"What if you've emptied the discretionary fund on emergencies that happen early in the month?" Nyota asked. "And what if we both see a need at the same time and think there is money to meet that need?"

"Looks like you have some homework to do," I said. "You should go through each area and find out what it would take to get you to a ten. Even if you move incrementally forward toward your ten, you'll see more balance and more effectiveness in your ministry. The next thing you should do is to consider what barriers in the past have kept you from being at a ten. When you've identified the barriers, see what you can do to keep those from getting in the way again."

"We can work on these," Nyota said. "What else do we have to do to bring our calling and our schedule into line?"

"Have you ever heard the concept of putting the big rocks in first?"

"I think I heard someone preach on that once," Francis said. "Is that where you put the important things in the schedule first?"

"Exactly," I said. "Hearing it in a sermon is different than putting it into practice in your life. If you want your calling to be effective, you need to understand what is necessary to protect and promote your calling and your covenant. Identify the three-to-six major things that do this and put those into your calendar first."

"Can you give us an example?" Nyota asked.

"For example, my wife and I sit down at the beginning of the year with our calendars, and put in a weekly date night. At the beginning of each month, we review all the activities and events, and coordinate what we are committing to. This keeps our covenant and our calling from clashing."

"We're not always so good at planning," Francis said. "So much comes up at the last minute. We deal with people who have unending emergencies."

"The beauty of the rocks in a jar idea is that you put in the major commitments first, then the next level of opportunities, then the everyday emergencies. When someone comes with an emergency, you may have to say, 'I'd love to help, but I have a commitment right now. How about we meet Tuesday afternoon, and I can give you my full attention?'"

"Does that really work?" Francis asked.

"If you have clarity around your calling and your covenant, then you'll soon find out," I answered.

"How do we decide what is a big rock and what's a medium rock?" Nyota asked.

I pulled out my binder and handed over a blank chart and a blank page. "Take a few minutes and use the blank page to list all the things you feel are taking up space in your life. Brainstorm, and list everything for now."

Nyota picked up the pen and wrote as the two of them called out things that took up space in their lives. "Now, let's take a look at this chart."

	URGENT	NONURGENT
I M P O R T A N T		
U N I M P O R T A N T		

"Can you think of some options that might fit in each box?" I asked. "For example, under *Urgent* and *Important,* you might have something like family emergencies or deadlines at work."

"Would we put date nights in there?" Francis asked.

"Yes, if you think they're urgent and important. What would you put in *Urgent* and *Unimportant*?"

"Anything that sucks our time and energy," Nyota answered. "Maybe phone messages or emails from charities, politicians, or people in the community who think we're the solution to their problems."

"Okay, write those down—and anything else you can think of. What about the *Nonurgent* and *Unimportant*?"

"Probably things that have no real value to our ministry or marriage," Francis said. "There's probably a few sports events or TV shows I could put in here."

"What about the last category?" I asked. "*Nonurgent,* yet *Important.*"

Nyota scribbled a few items on her sheet. "I'd put things that need planning, like holidays or retreats. Maybe time for visioning, budgeting, reading, and date nights."

"Very good. So, to finish this exercise, two questions. What are some urgent, unimportant things that you would like to spend less time doing? What are some nonurgent, important activities you want to prioritize more? You can talk about this at home."

Francis glanced up from the paper. "But sometimes things come up that we haven't even got on this list, and they seem pretty urgent. How do we tell our people they aren't important?"

"You'll need clarity around your calling and your covenant," I said. "Once that is in place, it will help you sort the rest of your list. There will be seasons when some things take on more urgency, and you'll have to work that into your monthly or weekly calendars. Just remember, you'll need space on your calendar for your spiritual and physical health. You'll need some margin so you can have space for emergencies."

"It would be nice to live outside a hurricane once in a while," Nyota said.

"One last thing for today," I said. "Sometimes we define our success too narrowly through the numbers associated with our work.

In churches, we might measure by attendance, giving, decisions for Christ, baptisms, small groups, or volunteers. Nonprofits might measure by grants, donations, volunteers, participants, etc. But what numbers might you unconsciously be using to determine the success of your marriage?"

"Are you saying that we might be defining our success by the number of causes and people we're supporting rather than the number of hours we spend nurturing our relationship?" Francis asked.

"I'm only asking," I said. "Sometimes, our success in some area opens up opportunities that are too irresistible to ignore. We extend ourselves more than our time or energy wisely permit. Our relationship is put on hold because we think there will be more time for each other later. I know you say you pray about all your decisions, but wisdom takes into account our limits, our responsibilities, our anxieties about making a difference, our support systems, and the counsel of others—like our spouse and friends."

Francis let out a sigh. "Yes, I admit it. Some days I'm so busy I don't even take the time to ask how this opportunity fits into my calling, or into God's design and desire for my life."

I took down a book from my shelf and opened it. "Peter Scazzero faced a similar time in his life. He was part of a growing ministry but realized it was failing because he didn't deal with what was happening inside himself. He came up with four characteristics to help him determine healthy planning. Your hearts may align with his, since I know you are working all out."

Emotionally Healthy Planning and Decision Making involves

- defining success as radically doing God's will;
- creating a space for heart preparation;
- praying for prudence;
- looking for God in our limits.[59]

"So, what happens if someone in authority over us decides we're the right person for some option, but we know that it's going to impact our marriage?" Francis asked.

"Never rush a *yes*," I said. "Take time to pray together until you both agree that this is right. Then decide what you're going to let go of so you can function with enough time and energy on the new option." I opened my Bible and flipped toward the book of Proverbs. "Proverbs 14:8 says, *'The wisdom of the prudent is to give thought to their ways.'* I flipped over the pages. "Proverbs 19:2 says, *'Desire without knowledge is not good—how much more will hasty feet miss the way?'*"

"Okay, we have some tools to work with on this," Nyota said. "I think the hard part is going to be communicating these changes with others who are used to us running around like whirling dervishes."

CALLING AND COMMUNICATION

> **"My best friend is the one who brings out the best in me." — Henry Ford**

Gerhard and Isabella walked through the door holding hands. "We came back," Gerhard announced. "We've been working on our raw spots, and we can see how our birth family experiences are impacting us now. I think we need to talk through how being married missionaries are two callings that can work together. Sometimes we get stuck."

"I think I'm the one who gets us stuck," Isabella said. "You know my situation, and how I fell into thinking that the mission, my marriage, and my family had trapped me into a life I couldn't escape. I don't know how to talk this through. Sometimes I get bizarre thoughts—like it would be easier to die. I don't have any plans or anything; I just get overwhelmed with emotion and don't know how to change anything."

"That's important to pay attention to," I said. "If you have a family history of someone taking their own life, or if there's been child abuse, violence, neglect, or trauma, it can prompt unwanted thoughts. Even losing friends this way or feeling unsupported in your current situation can raise these ideas for some. Getting overwhelmed with loneliness or hopelessness doesn't help. Falling into self-destructive behavior and wondering how far you can go isn't what you want. Having a chronic illness, being unable to access mental health care, struggling with relationship hostility, or even feeling the pressure of financial insecurity can stimulate thoughts you don't know how to process."

"It doesn't make sense," Isabella said. "I've followed God's call to engage in the Great Commission. I'm married, with a family. I'm usually healthy."

"There's actually no specific age, gender, race, or socioeconomic group that is more prone to this," I said. "Circumstances or traumatic life experiences may play a role, but this is important to talk through."

"How do I talk with Isabella so that she feels good about our calling?" Gerhard asked. "In our heads, we both know we're called to make disciples of Christ from all nations, but there are so many personal issues going on underneath that it's hard to talk about."

I nodded, acknowledging the frustration. "There are a few things to start with. Avoid getting defensive as if this is about you. Focus on naming Isabella's best intentions. Welcome her to remain open by pointing out something you appreciate about her, and support her in this willingness to share. Label out loud some of the strengths you see on display in her life. Offer empathy."

"That might be hard in the heat of the moment," Gerhard said, "but I can try. Anything else?"

"There's a practice that Thriving Relationship Coaches call 'wonder and look under.'[60] It's where you pause long enough before responding to something that is said and try to identify the feelings, fears, wounds, or dreams underneath whatever appears to be on the surface. For example, when Isabella comes to you questioning her calling, you might stop to consider what's going on under the surface for her at that moment. Don't be the typical man and try to solve it or fix it. Just listen for more."

"Easier said than done," Gerhard said. "I feel so helpless sometimes."

"Remember that your calling isn't about advising Isabella on how she can do life better. You are married to her for one purpose: to support and encourage her as God transforms her into becoming more and more like Christ. That isn't an easy journey for any of us."

"What does that look like?" Isabella asked.

"You may have heard it said that a very happy couple will use a 20:1 ratio in their positive and encouraging comments compared to their suggestive or corrective statements. You can still be happy if you pull off a 5:1 ratio. So, focus on thinking of positive, encouraging, and affirming statements throughout your day with whatever good you can see in front of you. This goes both ways for the two of you."

Gerhard leaned back on the loveseat and interlocked his fingers behind his head. "It makes sense that if I get demanding, then she'll get defensive. So, you're saying that I should only give unsolicited feedback only when I'm absolutely sure it is going to be helpful and productive."

"Yes! And use *I* statements combined with what you're feeling but do it without blaming."

"What if we get stuck talking about our pasts and all the wrongs that were done?" he asked.

"Deal with your pasts the best way you can," I said, "but focus on being present and future oriented. By the grace of God, you survived the challenges of the past. Now, you can say, 'Isabella, I see that your struggle in the past has given you a drive to care for others, a determination to bring your best to the challenges you face, and a compassionate heart for the needy. I'm so glad that our calling is better because you bring all that to what God is doing in us and through us.'"

"Wow! I never thought that my past could be seen positively like that," Isabella said.

"If you see and assume the best in others, that can bring out the best in you as well," I said. "When you're wanting to communicate, make sure you're relaxed in mind and body. Don't come all uptight and tense, and expect your partner to accept things well. If an affectionate touch is appropriate, it might help ease the situation."

"I like the touch idea," Gerhard said, smiling.

"I can see how my tendency to blame Gerhard for everything I feel doesn't help our communication a lot," Isabella said. "If our communication is going well, we'll be more confident in our calling."

"Make sure you take full responsibility for your part in whatever has happened," I said. "Remember, your partner is their own unique self.

Don't expect them to be you. Don't expect them to read your mind or to feel the way you feel."

"I tend to like face-to face-communication, but I guess it doesn't matter whether we send texts, emails, or post-it notes," Isabella said. "As long as we're connecting, it doesn't matter who is ultimately right on something."

"Well said. Developing a strong and healthy partnership is more important than being right. Be humble, gracious, patient, and understanding. It all helps keep the relationship happier."

"Sometimes I don't do so well in accepting Gehard's input when I'm hungry, angry, lonely, or tired," Isabella admitted. "I tend to get critical and defensive at those times."

"You're in this together as a team," I said. "Take some time to pause, get centered, and even take a short break if you need to before re-engaging. Try to stay curious through open-ended questions."

Isabella leaned over and kissed Gerhard on the cheek. "Sorry, babe. I know we're in this calling together. As long as our communication stays good, I think I can keep believing it."

CALLING AND AUTHORITY

"No friendship is an accident." — O. Henry

Hailey and Simon walked through my door for their appointment, but both of them were on their phones talking to individuals somewhere else. Simon waved hello to me, then wandered to the window and continued talking to someone clearly in trouble. Hailey hovered in the doorway, facing away with one hand over her ear as she whispered to another troubled soul. Simon was the first to pocket his phone and slump down onto the loveseat.

"Busy day," I noted, nodding toward Hailey.

"Story of our life," Simon replied. "This is part of our issue with each other. We never have space to talk. Even in the car someone is calling. We're so busy dealing with other people's problems, we don't have time to deal with our own."

"And what might be the problem you have today?" I asked.

Simon leaned forward and whispered, "It's Hailey's father. That's who she's on the phone with. He feels like, somehow, he's been called to be our guardian or authority. We've been married fourteen years—and doing this work for eight—yet he still tries to tell us what he thinks our calling is."

"Did you two elope or something?" I asked.

"Almost," Simon said. "Her father wanted her to marry a youth pastor in his church, and so a lot of our relationship happened without him knowing how serious it was. We met in counseling classes, hung around at school, and since we were in another town, shared dinners while we studied. The first time I met her folks was when we went to tell them we were engaged."

"That might do it," I said. "Should we wait for Hailey?"

"She doesn't want her dad knowing we're coming to you for help," Simon said. "He thinks he's the only advisor in our life. He's the one who suggested we needed outside help, but we realize he was meaning his help. I think Hailey ends up telling him too many of our personal things, and that keeps him trying to rescue her." Simon rose and gently put his hand on Hailey's shoulder. She nodded and ended her call.

"Sorry about that," she said, standing in front of the desk. "Dad was worried about whether Simon was encouraging me enough in my calling. He's almost as protective as Simon's board."

"Intrusive is more like it," Simon said.

"Sounds like we have authorities who aren't sure where the boundaries are."

"I don't know if it's boundaries," Simon said. "It's like they doubt our calling and keep trying to steer us in another direction."

"It's an interesting thing to come under an authority who pays your salary," I said. "You might be sure that your calling is the Great Commission, and you might be sure that God has equipped you and directed you to express your calling in what you're doing, but if you haven't got authorities who embrace you as the right people in the right place, you may have to consider whether there is another option."

"How do we even talk to these people about how we feel?" Simon asked.

"You can interact by changing just a few phrases," I said. "One suggestion is that you start off any comments you make by saying, 'I'm puzzled.'[61] For example, 'I'm puzzled that you are so positive God has something else for me to do. Do you mind letting me know why you are so confident of this?'"

"I suppose that's one way of lowering the temperature," Simon said.

"The other thing that Hailey might say to her father is something like, 'Dad, I notice that you still feel free to direct my life even after I've been gone for fourteen years. I prefer that you let Simon and I figure out the next steps in God's calling on our life.'"

"Yikes! Are you trying to get me kicked off the inheritance list?" Hailey asked. "No one talks to Dad like that. He ran his own business, and everyone knew who was boss."

"The good thing for you is that you don't work for your dad, and he's not your boss," I said. "As for the inheritance list, nothing I can do about that one. I'm thinking that perhaps your dad would have more confidence in letting you make your own decisions if you really did start making your own decisions with Simon."

"Have you heard about the Ladder of Integrity?"[62] I asked, sliding a diagram toward them. Both shook their heads, so I explained it. "It's a way for you to discover what's going on inside you in terms of values—so you can assert yourself in a respectful way without blaming your authorities. So much of conflict is about what is going on inside us instead of what's going on inside the other person."

"I see ten phrases on the page," Hailey said. "What are we supposed to do with those?"

"That is going to be your homework assignment," I said. "You finish each sentence, and then put them into a paragraph to deal with an issue. For example, let's imagine you are going to talk to your dad about his interference in your sense of call, and Simon is going to talk to his board chair about their interference in his work. Why don't you read them so we can get our brains pumped and ready to go?"

Hailey lifted her page off the desk. "I don't know about this. Writing it out is one thing, but thinking of my dad reading this sends shivers down my back. Simon may be out of a job if he goes through with his."

"Do you trust God if this is his call on your life?" I asked.

Hailey sighed and nodded. "Okay. I see that phrases 1-4 are about what is going on in me. Numbers 5-8 are about what I value. And 9-10 is about what I hope. Sounds harmless right now."

1. Right now the issue on my mind is...
2. My part in this is...
3. My need in this issue is...
4. My feelings about this are...
5. This issue is important to me because I value... and I violate that value when...
6. I am willing/not willing to...
7. One thing I could do to improve the situation is...
8. The most important thing I want you to know is...
9. I think my honest sharing will benefit our relationship by...
10. I hope and look forward to...

"Once we write all this out, then we put it into the form of a letter. Is that right?" Hailey asked.

"Exactly!" I said. "If there are elephants in the room, secrets you are keeping to yourself, or grudges you are carrying, then it's important to keep your communication open. If you have a calling that you're convinced God has given you, then it's wise to have your authorities fully supporting you. If they don't, it may be a good time to re-evaluate where you should be next."

"I guess the most important thing is that we are in this together," Simon said.

"Yes. Committed to covenant and calling."

QUAGMIRE FOUR

Family

> "Come, let's be a comfortable
> couple and take care of each other!
> How glad we shall be, that we have
> somebody we are fond of always,
> to talk to and sit with."
> — Charles Dickens

If any one quagmire is going to create conflict between ministry and marriage, it will be the issue of family. The larger the family, the more potential there is for stress between the expectations at home and the expectations in ministry. Issues like parenting styles and investment, household rules, the impact of in-laws, finances, roles in the home, and even cultural differences can stretch the limits of our harmony.

Seasoned leaders navigate most of the rapids for family conflict while they're younger, but the patterns we establish early in our relationships often surface again later with new rapids, whirlpools, and waterfalls that mean portaging in times when our children are adolescents or transitioning out of the home. We may need to re-examine the routines we've established, routines that once worked for us.

FAMILY AND PARENTING

Sam and Hannah arrived together, but Hannah sat in a single chair and left the loveseat to Sam. "How did you do in finding and affirming each other's strengths this past week?" I asked.

Hannah curled her lip. "Hard to do that when he's busy all the time."

Sam scooted forward to the front of the loveseat. "And why am I busy all the time? I'm looking after our kids and trying to do a full-time job."

"Well, it so happens that I, too, am working," Hannah said, "and since I'm just starting out, I end up putting in overtime."

"How are we going to sort this out?" Sam asked. "I don't even know where to start."

I pulled out my pen and scratch pad to take notes. "You are definitely in a difficult spot," I said. "If you received three wishes for your family, what would you choose?"

Sam rubbed his forehead with a knuckled fist and wrinkled his brow. "First, I'd have Hannah come back home." He looked toward Hannah. "That seems like an obvious choice. Second, I wish I knew how to communicate my love to Hannah in a way that she could appreciate and accept. Third, I wish I could take all her pain and replace it with peace."

"You couldn't handle my pain," Hannah said. "You think that quoting a few verses, watching a few sermons, and getting through a few chats are going to undo everything that I've had to put up with. For some reason, apparently, I didn't pick up the parenting gene."

"Hannah, what about you?" I asked. "What three wishes would you bring to your relationship?"

She sprang from her chair and paced the room, stopping to look out the window. "That's a question Sam should have asked me before we got married. Pregnancy was hell. I've never felt so alone in my life." She spun on her heels and stood behind the love seat, looking down on her husband. "I wish I could do so much of this relationship over again. I wish my past nightmares wouldn't keep paralyzing me every time Sam comes near." She put a hand on Sam's shoulder. "I wish you could take my pain as well."

"What is it about these things that are meaningful to you?" I asked. "Sam, you first."

Sam laid his hand on Hannah's, and she let it rest there for a moment before backing away. "Having Hannah home was my first wish.

None of us are functioning well without her. I don't even know where everything is. I don't know where the right clothes are for the right child. I never learned to make the right meals." He stood and faced Hannah. "I don't know how to keep the kids from crying at bedtimes when they want their mother. I bring in sitters and friends, but that doesn't help anything."

"I think my question was, why is Hannah being home so meaningful for you? Let's just focus on your first wish for now."

Sam leaned back against the loveseat and opened his arms in helplessness. "I pledged my life to you. I had kids with you. I feel incomplete without you. You're my whole world."

"Can you receive that?" I asked Hannah.

"There's just more to this relationship than all that," she said. "When I said I wish I could do this relationship all over again, it's not that I want to be with someone else. It would be meaningful to me if we could somehow connect deeply beyond the quick hug goodbye. I feel like I lost you somewhere. We used to laugh, go on adventures, have fun, dream about changing the world together."

"What gets in the way of you experiencing these things?" I asked. "Hannah, why don't you pick up where you left off?"

She kicked off her shoes, stepped onto the cushioned loveseat, and sat on the arm. "What gets in the way of us dreaming and having fun together? Mostly work, kids, chores, schedules, and money."

"And you, Sam?"

"Yeah, I guess that's what I'm saying, too, when I say I want you back home. I still think we have a chance to dream, only with a few kids tagging along to fill out the dreams. I think we have just let others determine our life for us up until now."

"You let others put their rocks in your jar so that you had no room for your own," I said. "So, what does this barrier require from you in order to remove it? And I'm not speaking about the kids. There are no refunds for those little love projects."

"I could rework my job description to make it more reasonable," Sam said, "as long as I could get the board to understand why my commitment to covenant is as important as my commitment to the commission."

"I am not ready to quit my job, if that's what you expect," Hannah said. "I feel like I'm coming off as the bad guy in this relationship just because I need a little fulfillment in my life. I've said it before. I did not get hired by Sam's board to be his errand boy. Life in this place is expensive. We needed money. Now we need more."

"Is there a different way you can see or respond to this barrier to generate different results?" I asked.

"If I did move home," Hannah said, "we'd need some clear understanding about how we're going to parent together. We need that even if we're apart. I can't have you marching in and making up a bunch of rules that you expect me to enforce. Rules I don't always agree with. We need to sit down and talk through what is best for us and for the kids. Even they need some say."

"I could probably do some of my work via distance learning," Sam said. "There are options we never used to have. I could counsel or tutor online. I like the face-to-face and on-campus busyness, but I could make adjustments. One of the freshman girls volunteered to help with the kids whenever we need it."

I set down the pen I'd been using to take notes. "If you saw this barrier as wisdom pointing you toward the solution, what is it inviting you to change—inside and out?"

Sam kicked off his shoes, stepped onto the loveseat, and sat on the arm facing Hannah. "If I took a sabbatical, maybe it would give us time to figure things out. I could still write a bit."

Hannah shook her head vigorously. "No! You're not giving up your position. I see how thrilled you are to pour into those students, and we need the money for the mortgage—and for the kids' sports. Maybe we could work out different shifts so one of us is usually around for the kids."

"What about us?" Sam asked.

"Yeah, I think we still have some work to do on us," Hannah said.

"What is one inspired action you can take toward your wish?"

"We can talk to our bosses to see about adjusting our schedules," Sam said. "It may take some time, but if we had something to work toward, it might hold us through in the meantime."

"I still say we need to sort out our parenting styles before I step back into things," Hannah said. "I'm willing to go for a walk on Saturday and maybe Tuesday evening to talk this through. I also want to start dreaming again about what we can do to bring some adventure back into our marriage."

"It's a start," I said. "Go do it."

FAMILY AND RULES

"You are braver than you believe, stronger than you seem, and smarter than you think." —Christopher Robin

Esther and Phil had missed a few sessions due to scheduling conflicts, and it was clear right away that things hadn't improved during their time away. Esther chose one of the two chairs near the desk, and Phil sank into the loveseat.

"Took everything I have to get that lug away from his laptop," she started. "I'm tired of making excuses for him to everyone in the family."

Phil sat forward. "Well, not everyone in the family needs to hear your excuses. I'm tired of all the rules you've been using to put me in a straightjacket. I feel like you're trying to impose your daddy's rules on me, as if I'm some kind of child."

"If you'd stop acting like a child, I wouldn't have to treat you like one," she said. "Now, can we get on with this session?"

"Sounds like we're already underway," I said.

"What do you mean?" she asked.

"Have you heard of Transactional Analysis?" I asked.

"If it wasn't on the seminary reading list, then I don't think I have," she said.

"The idea of TA is that all of us are acting out one of three roles. We are acting as Parent, Adult, or Child." I flipped open my binder and pulled out a chart, which I passed over to her.

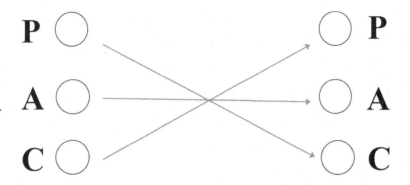

"The theory says that two people are always acting in one of these ways. The ideal for a married couple in leadership is that they are acting like two mature adults in the way they respect and treat each other. They speak in calm and thoughtful tones. They work for each other's best interests."

Esther slid the paper back toward me. "I don't need you ganging up on me, you hear? I know what you're doing. Saying I'm acting more like his mother than his wife. Being a wife doesn't mean I have to grovel and slither on my belly just to make him happy."

"I'm actually focusing on the way Phil is responding to you."

"About time," she said.

"When you start putting rules on him, he immediately becomes like a child and gives you no choice but to take on the parent role. What makes you think rules are going to get him to do what you want him to do?"

"They worked in my family, and my staff sure responds to them," Esther said.

"Too bad they didn't work for God."

"What do you mean?"

"Think Garden of Eden, or The Big Ten."

"Well, our rules were different," Esther said. "We had those ten, plus a lot of unwritten rules."

"God's rules were designed to help his people thrive."

"Well, ours sure weren't."

"So, what kind of rules did you live under?"

"For one, girls are to be seen but not heard. We were dolled up and paraded around on Sundays with big smiles on our faces." Esther rose, crossed her arms over her chest, and paced around the Persian carpet. "I tried telling my younger brother he shouldn't talk or draw attention to himself, but Mom told me to hush and learn my place. Daddy told us that all girls knew how to do with their tongues was to gossip, blame, and slander."

"That must have been hard," Phil said.

"It's harder when I'm thinking you don't want me talking," Esther said. "It's also hard when I go to conventions, and they tell me to go sit in with the pastors' wives. I even heard one minister tell his buddy that he hoped his wife wasn't in there sharing all their secrets with the other gossip girls. I feel like I always have to prove myself, but nobody wants to listen when I try."

"I trust you're learning to talk directly to the people who need to know what you know," I said. "That you are unlocking the secrets you've hidden inside. That you are finding a trustworthy person somewhere to talk to about anything and everything."

"I'm still learning how to do that," Esther said. "That's why I need to know Phil is with me and not hiding away with his own little secrets."

I flipped open my binder and slid a handout over to Phil. "I'm assuming you're practicing a few listening skills to help Esther with her talking. Perhaps you can say these four things out loud so that Esther hears your heart when she wants to talk."

He slid the page over so Esther could see better.

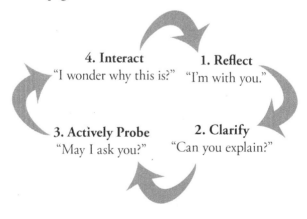

4. **Interact**
"I wonder why this is?"

1. **Reflect**
"I'm with you."

3. **Actively Probe**
"May I ask you?"

2. **Clarify**
"Can you explain?"

"Reflect, Clarify, Actively Probe, Interact."[63] Phil turned the page over, but seeing nothing else, he scanned the diagram again. "Sounds like stuff I've heard before," he said.

"Good! Then it won't be a surprise to know that Esther needs you to keep practicing these things so she can learn to talk with you in a way that you appreciate. Good questions are how we humans connect."

"I'll try to make it worth your while," Esther said, winking at Phil.

"What other rules do you think are still impacting your relationships now?" I asked.

"I know you talk a lot about feelings in here," Esther said, "but our family wasn't much into letting our feelings show. At least, not so Mom and Dad could see them. There was plenty of emotion from Dad, raising his voice and all, so the rest of us didn't need to contribute a whole lot."

"My family was similar," Phil said. "I heard everywhere that you couldn't trust feelings or that feelings were the last things to think about. I think every Christian had that drilled into their head. I learned in seminary that we were like God because we were emotional beings who feel, volitional beings who choose, rational beings who think, and personal beings who long and desire. It didn't make sense to me then 'cause I felt like I had to deny part of who I was made to be."[64]

"You'll probably notice that one emotion you experience all too frequently is fear," I said. "Just like the Pharisees whom Jesus faced, you probably use rules to create layers to protect you from your fears. When you go home this week, you should list your fears, and then write out all the rules or actions you do to protect yourself from those fears."

"I think we have another rule in our family," Esther said. "I think 'don't trust' is pretty common. When I see Phil on his computer, and then find those images, I see half a dozen marriages that have dissolved in our extended family. I don't want that humiliation and pain, but what can I do to change the inevitable?"

"You can be wise," I said. "Wise people own their own stuff. They embrace it and adjust. They show remorse over their own mistakes and empathize with others in regards to their own attitudes and behaviors."[65]

"We had a rule in our family that still paralyzes me," Phil said. "We weren't allowed to choose. Mom would ask me whether I wanted to wear the blue sweater or the green one to school. I'd say green, and she would say, 'No, the blue one goes better with your eyes.'" He lowered his head into his hands. "One time dad asked me whether I wanted to play football or soccer. I said football, and he said, 'No, you're too frail. You'll get hurt. Anyway, it's cheaper to play soccer.'"

"So, how do you think that impacted you and your relationships?" I asked.

He lifted his head, then shook it back and forth slowly. "I never learned to respect myself or my choices. I always fear those in authority and what they might choose for me. I don't know what to do with the consequences that come my way when I do make a choice." He looked toward Esther. "Sometimes, you terrify me with the rules you impose and the consequences that might come with those rules. I don't think I'll ever measure up to your expectations."

"I guess I talk a lot about grace with people at the church, but I don't really know how to apply it at home," she said. "I almost dread coming home at the end of the day. I'm just not sure how you are going to betray me or let me down."

"It's harder than we think some days," I said. "If we've grown up in a shame-based culture, where acceptance is rare, and we hear messages saying there is something wrong with us; if we feel we don't measure up; if we can never seem to prove our worth; if we're seen as the problem because we think there's a problem; if our family only focuses on head knowledge over heart knowledge; and if image is more important than integrity, then we are thirsty for grace."

"So, you think we're okay?" Esther asked.

"Neither one of you is a victim," I said. "You're partners, designated to help each other thrive. It sounds like old rules are getting in the way of a new relationship. Take this week to sort through the rules you've absorbed and how those rules are impacting you inside—as to the choices, feelings, and expectations you carry. Consider then how that rule is impacting your relationship and come up with one or two specific steps you're going to take to overcome that rule."

"Okay, I think I've got it," Esther said. "Respect is giving Phil space, letting him be his own person, not taking every disagreement personally, listening to each other, giving him the benefit of the doubt once in a while, telling the truth, forgiving mistakes, checking in to see how my schedule is impacting him, and then being respectful in the way I speak and react."

"Not sure where that list comes from," I said, "but it sounds like you understand family."

FAMILY AND IN-LAWS

"The highest happiness on earth is marriage."
— William Lyon Phelps

Hailey and Simon settled into the loveseat, both scrolling through their phones and texting others not in the room. It seemed that they didn't even notice my presence, so I waited for them to look up. Simon glanced up first and then nudged Hailey with his elbow.

"Family crisis," Hailey said.

"That's code for Hailey's daddy wanting her immediate attention," Simon said. "When we cancelled our holiday, he went out of his way to book us another option near to where he lives. He also invited some other family members with whom we don't always see eye-to-eye."

"I think it's just a difference in the way our two families communicate," Hailey said. "With Mom gone, Dad feels protective. He likes to be involved in our lives. He does that for all his kids. Simon's mom and dad are like ghosts who expect us to read their minds when they want us to connect. Our family talks about everything openly. Simon's family treats every issue as if it's locked up in Fort Knox with all the gold bullion."

"I think the issue of faith impacts things as well," Simon added. "Hailey's dad was a successful businessman who didn't have time for matters of faith, whereas my folks practically lived in the church and are totally committed to what's happening there. If they had their way, we would live in the same community with them and set up our counseling practice in the church offices."

Hailey's phone buzzed. She picked it up, glanced at it, and set it back down. "I think that neither of us realized we were marrying into a family package. Both families have different values, expectations around children, beliefs, desires for how holidays are spent, and convictions about our career choices."

"I think Hailey's dad deliberately violates our boundaries to let me know he's still the real man in Hailey's life. Hailey thinks it's unintentional. I think it's very much intentional."

Hailey shook her head back and forth. "No, not at all. Dad used to work all the time when we were growing up. I think he feels guilty about never being around, and he's trying to make up for it. He's got a good heart."

"That's exactly why he reminds you on every phone call whether you or your sister is higher up on the inheritance list? Of course, your brother is number one and can do no wrong. But your place is totally dependent on whether you're keeping in touch, performing acts of service, and listening to his advice."

"It's a family joke," Hailey said. "It was going on before we were married."

I held up my hand and opened my binder. "It's easy to get stuck in loyalty conflicts—in jealousy, insecurity, and unresolved family disputes from years ago. You are your own family now, and you can create a ton of unnecessary suffering by prolonging these conflicts. Let's look at how we can turn our thoughts around."

"I agree," Hailey said. "It's easy to get trapped by our thoughts. How do we change all this?"

"You need to start by determining which thought you want to change," I said. "Simon, why don't you start?"

Simon stifled a yawn and slapped his cheeks. "Sorry, late party, not much sleep. I guess my thought would be that my father-in-law is a busybody."

"Okay, what emotion arises when you think of your father-in-law?"

"Just one? Okay, I get intimidated. I get angry. I get anxious." Simon ran his fingers through his hair. "I also love his generosity, his commitment to his family, and his strong business sense. It's confusing."

"Let's focus on questioning some of our negative thoughts about our in-laws," I said.[66] "You believe your father-in-law is an intrusive, overbearing busybody. Can you absolutely know that's true? What happens when you believe this thought? Who would you be without this thought?"

"If I have to question everything I think, then what can I know for sure?" he asked. "I guess I want to reposition myself as enough for Hailey, as having enough to provide for Hailey."

"It's hard to do that inner work when we are in conflict," I said. "Let's ask another line of questions. When is the opposite true? When are you sure your father-in-law isn't just being an intrusive, overbearing busybody? When have you acted like an intrusive, overbearing busybody toward him? Or to yourself? Or to Hailey?"

"This is no longer fun," Simon said. "Why don't you try this with Hailey and my family?"

I laid my pen down on the desk. "One more step and we're done. Based on what you now realize, what new thought might you embrace toward Hailey's father, a thought that might be more helpful in your relationship with him and with Hailey?"

"I get it," Simon said. "Jesus told us not to judge, or we will be judged. He also told us that we need to love one another in the same way he loved us. It's not very good to be counseling others if I can't take counsel for myself."

"How can we deal with the issue Hailey's father is concerned with? After all, wasn't it your father, Simon, who first intervened to suggest you needed outside help?"

"Yeah! Wasn't that weird?" Hailey said.

"At least I'm not making an idol out of my family," Simon said.

"No argument there," Hailey said. "With everyone else in your life, you haven't got time to think of us."

"That's not what I meant," Simon said.

"I know," Hailey said. "You're busy trying to break your youth from their idolatrous obsessions with sports, sex, technology, work, money, and power." She glanced at her husband's open mouth and then put her finger over her lips. "Sorry, that slipped out. You know I'm with you. You make a big difference for all those kids. I just wish I could slide into your schedule somewhere."

"Perhaps we could solve the issue for Simon's father and for you as well," I said. "Remember the concept of putting the big rocks into the jar first?"

"Yes, we take the most important things for our marriage, then our ministry, then our family and community, and put them on our schedule," Simon said. "Then we take the next level of things, like all the stuff we do with the youth, and put it into whatever slots are left. Finally, we add any extras."

I nodded. "If you've already put holidays, retreats, sabbaths, or whatever else is needed into the schedule to keep you close, and then layered the other things in afterward, you can assure your father that you have a plan. You can also assure Hailey's father that you are taking care of her needs. And then make sure you have space for both fathers if that is important to you. You might save yourself a lot of phone calls with just a little planning."

"I guess we need to work on our grace," Simon said.

"Yes. Keep sharing those messages of welcome and acceptance. Cherish the relationship and bathe it in affirmation. Be consistent. If you have rules for your relationship, agree on them together, and state them clearly to anyone they impact. Speak truthfully and clearly. Speak from the heart. Guard your integrity."

"Maybe you can talk with my dad next time he calls," Hailey said.

FAMILY AND FINANCES

> **"Do what you can, with what you have, where you are." —Teddy Roosevelt**

Ben and Susan arrived with Ben lugging in a cardboard box. "It's all our paperwork for income tax," Ben said. "We were at the financial advisor, sorting out how we should be setting ourselves up for the future."

"Smart idea," I said. "Finances are near the top when it comes to conflicts that destroy relationship."

"Why do you think that is?" Susan asked.

"What have you discovered so far in your own relationship?"

Ben set his box down on the floor by the loveseat, dropped his coat over the back, and sank down into the cushions. "I think part of our issue is circumstantial. As you know, we were both in seminary, working on the side to pay our tuition. There wasn't much left over. Then the kids arrived one after the other while I was studying, and we had loans to deal with. Our church plant was small, and there wasn't much income, except a little for food, rent, and debt repayment."

Susan shifted, and I looked in her direction. "There's also the issue of who gets to decide on spending. Ben came from a family with a little more money while my family has always had to be thrifty. Ben is now earning money, but we're both working hard. He feels he should have some extra money to buy books, have fun, and spend on his pet projects." She twirled an earring as she glanced at her husband. "I've been given the task of managing our budget, but it always seems that I'm running short. When we do fight, it does seem to come back to this issue more often than not."

"We both sit down at the start of the year to set up our budget," Ben said. Facing me, he pulled out a black financial ledger and opened it up on the desk. "We have ten categories to manage." He pointed to each column as he focused on it.

"*Fixed expenses*, like tithe, rent, insurance, and utilities like electricity, water, gas, internet, phone.

We have *variable expenses* like groceries, household supplies, transportation (with gas and maintenance), clothing, personal care items, and entertainment for our date nights and travel.

We have *debt* payments in the third column to pay off credit cards, student loans, and car loans.

In the fourth column, we have our *savings* for retirement, emergencies and a little for the kids' college fund.

This fifth column is for *insurance*—things like health, life, car, etc.

The sixth column is for our *kids*. Things like childcare if we need it, or education expenses— school tuition, fees, and supplies.

The seventh column is for *healthcare*. This is anything not covered by insurance. Like prescriptions.

The eighth column is our *recreation* fund. It includes hobbies, outings, vacations, and subscriptions.

Ninth, we have *miscellaneous* expenses. Things like gifts, holidays, house maintenance, and membership fees for the gym if we ever get some free time.

Tenth. *Taxes.* Income tax, and any other taxes that come our way."

"We keep our receipts, manage every penny, and Susan tracks it all."

"Impressive!" I said. "You've solved half your conflicts just by having a budget. Have you considered another column where you and Sharon are given a couple hundred dollars each for discretionary spending? This would be money you wouldn't have to keep receipts for. It might include a coffee, a haircut, or a gift for a friend."

"That would be so wonderful," Susan said. "Sometimes I'm out with friends and things get awkward because I'm not sure if it's okay to buy a coffee for them, or to get a pedicure. Once we pay off our debts, things will get easier, but it's tough right now."

"What are some of your friction points over money?" I asked.

"I'm a bit more of a spender than Susan," Ben said. "On myself, and what I like. But she's more generous with others. We have crazy arguments like, if there's a need to sponsor a child, or to support a missionary, or to give to a project at church. I tell her there's nothing in the budget, and she says we can take it from our tithe, and I tell her that a tithe is only for the church, and we have no room left for giving more."

"It sounds like you are at least talking through your financial issues," I said. "You might expand your discussion around finances—beyond just having a budget—by setting up some goals, expectations, and desires before you put down the numbers each year. You might also want to set up a fund where you can put extra money that comes your way. This could be used for your generosity, or for dreams. You have a financial advisor, which is good, but there are going to be misunderstandings that arise if you allow money to be your master rather than your servant."

"What do you mean by that?" Ben asked.

"Take the area of generosity, for example. You tithe to your church. Do you do that out of obligation—because you feel you have to? In order to obey? Do you prioritize a percentage to give first, save a bit second, and live on the rest? Or do you give out of thankfulness for what God has given, trusting that he knows your current and future needs? Can you give thoughtfully, with consideration for the needs of your community in line with 2 Corinthians 9:6-11? Talking this through ahead of time can affect your whole attitude toward money, as long as you're both on the same page."

Ben nodded. "I think Susan feels trapped because I'm the one earning the money, and she's the one managing it. Our unequal earning power sets up disparities and a sense of imbalance. I don't see it that way, but I think sometimes she resents my ability to work and earn."

"I do sometimes feel insecure and resentful," Susan said. "You not only have more income, you have way more debt because of your studies. I agreed to give you the freedom to push on with those studies, and to take on the public role at the church. I love our community. It's managing the expectations, more than the dollars, that stifles me."

"I told you we could adjust our debt repayments," Ben said. "I told you I could take that part-time job to earn some more income to cover the debts. But you told me I need to be available for the kids."

"And me," Susan said. "Sometimes, I see the big picture, and it looks like forever before we'll get out from under the pressures. I don't want to have unrealistic expectations around our lifestyle, or spending, or travel; but sometimes I need space to breathe. I get overwhelmed by frustration and disappointment when another dream gets dashed because there's not enough money."

"It does seem that at least you have a roadmap," I said. "Without it you would even have more difficulties and disorganization to deal with. Your conflicts would be even more intense. A blessing is that you don't have any financial activities that might erode your trust in this relationship."

"Meaning?" Ben asked.

"You're not off gambling, earning and spending money secretively, carrying undisclosed debts, or spending outside your budget," I said. "Your open books show transparency, and that is crucial for a healthy relationship going forward."

"So, we shouldn't be having conflicts when it comes to money," Susan said.

"There will always be conflict when you have a difference in philosophy around money," I said. "I see you haven't protected yourself against possibilities like job loss, unexpected medical expenses, or economic downturns. I hear your church is a beautiful community to work in, but it helps to realize that there are many things that happen with a board, with leaders, or with circumstances that could impact you."

"I think we're okay in that area," Ben said.

"Okay," I said. "What would happen if this worship leader you were singing with looked differently at the relationship than you intended? What if she made a complaint to the board when you backed off? What if the board had members who cared more about the reputation of the church than about hearing your heart and healing the wounds? You could suddenly be out of a job and short of income for your nice budget."

"Do you think that could happen?" Susan asked.

"Being in ministry is not as predictable as it used to be," I said. "There's a lot of pressure on administrative leaders to guard against lawsuits. There's a lot in the news about senior male executives who take advantage of women. Our culture is primed to believe the worst about those in power. You never know what can happen. And imagine the impact on your own relationship if that process plays out?"

"I'm not sure I wanted to hear all that," Ben said. "I felt much better talking with my financial advisor."

"I am here for one reason," I said. "To help you grow your relationship so that it thrives. I'm just saying that finances can thwart that healthy growth in ways you can't imagine or prepare for. When the two of you are talking about your lives, make sure you focus at least some of your attention on the details around stewardship, generosity, budgeting, and financial planning for your future. Whether you realize it or not, there are small eyes watching your attitude toward the resources you have, and they will learn a lot more from you than from a future financial advisor."

FAMILY AND ROLES

> **"The greatest marriages are built on teamwork. A mutual respect, a healthy dose of admiration, and a never-ending portion of love and grace."[67]** — Fawn Weaver

Francis and Nyota stepped into the office and moved into a dance pose. Nyota nudged her phone to put on a lively tune, and they whirled around the small space on the Persian carpet. They'd clearly been practicing, and I was impressed. "Nice moves," I said.

"Don't you be thinking you can cut in," Francis said. "This woman is all mine."

"I see that. Does this mean our time here is coming to an end?"

Nyota broke out of the dance and moved to the loveseat. "I think we still need a few sessions. We're kind of sorting out what we will and won't do in our ministries, but now we're having a struggle trying to figure out who is going to do what at home. We always had someone in our home who would pick up, clean, or make food. Now we realize that, by reclaiming our home, we are also reclaiming all the work that needs to get done."

"I think you've moved into what Dr. Howard Hendricks says is a dance of its own.[68] In this dance, we realize that we are unconsciously incompetent—we don't know what we don't know. When we move into awareness, like you are now, we become consciously incompetent. We become aware that we don't know something, and we admit it. At this point, we begin to learn the skills we didn't know—we move into a conscious competence. Lastly, our skills become such a part of who we are that we move into an unconscious competence—we don't even think about what we know. We just live it out. Kind of like the dance moves I saw you two using a moment ago."

"Sounds like a great idea," Nyota said, "but can you teach us the steps?"

I took out my faithful binder and passed them two copies of a handout called 'Relationship Check-In.' "These are questions you can ask each other to get the dance going. You can improvise by adding more questions about the specific things you are dealing with, like chores. Let's give it a whirl. Nyota, you ask the first question, and Francis will answer it. Then he'll ask you the same question, and you can answer it."

Nyota nodded and held the paper closer. "Francis, honey, when have you been feeling the happiest and most connected?" She shared a sly grin. "Apart from our last time together."

"Too bad," he said. "That was going to be easy. I guess when we rented those bikes at the park last Saturday and just did something impulsive. I felt like when we first started dating. It was a great day." He lifted his paper. "Nyota, darling, love of my life, when have you been feeling the happiest and most connected? Apart from our last time together and our bike ride?"

Nyota furrowed her brow and wrapped her arms around her drawn up knees. "I'm thinking that I felt that way when you brought home the groceries and that ice cream last Wednesday. It kind of got my juices flowing if you know what I mean."

"Sounds like you two are learning some great moves in this relationship," I said. "Let's look at the next questions."

"When have you been feeling the most distant?" Francis asked.

Nyota released her legs and set her elbows on her knees, chin in hands. "Last night. I felt very distant when we tried to sort out the chores for the coming week, and you made that comment about laundry not being a man's job."

Francis stood, hands on hips. "And you said that cooking, making the bed, raking the leaves, sweeping the floor, cleaning the garage, balancing the budget, shopping for groceries, washing the car, and doing hospitality for guests was no longer the woman's job."

"Don't forget washing the windows, taking out the compost, weeding the garden, buying clothes, changing tires, and all the other stuff I listed. So, when did you feel the most distant?"

"Same time," Francis said. "There's got to be a way we can sort this out."

"How about making a game of it?" I suggested. "You could list all the chores on pieces of paper. One on each. Then at a set time, you could draw them out of a bowl to see what you get to do for the week. Each of you would take half, and then you would be responsible to figure out when you would get them done."

"It's bizarre enough that it just might work," Nyota said. "Both of us grew up in more conservative, traditional homes where our moms did most of the chores around the house. We took it for granted, but I don't have time for all that while I'm also working. Francis thinks that everything inside the house is mine to do, plus the gardens. He handles the cars."

"I do other things as well, once in a while," Francis said.

"Change is hard," I said. "Making a game of it might help. You're a new family, and you get to establish how the roles will work out."

Nyota motioned with her hand. "I'll read the next question. What would you love for me to do or say more of?"

"Do I have to answer that in front of the doc?" Francis asked. "Seriously, back to the last question before this. Can we modify things a bit?

"What do you mean?" Nyota asked.

"What if we wrote out all the chores and then chose four or five each, one at a time, that we were willing to do every week? Maybe we'd choose them because we're gifted in that area—like finances—or because we're used to doing those things. Then we could randomly draw the rest."

"I like that," Nyota said.

"The idea is yours, free of charge," I said.

I rummaged through my file folder and drew out another piece of paper. "Here's a starter list of possible chores you can work with. Maybe you can create individual slips for each option, make your choices, and then draw the rest. If there are some that don't apply you can discard them."

"Wow! I didn't realize there was this much to do around the house," Francis said. "Have you really been doing all this kind of stuff?"

Nyota scanned her list for a moment. "Not all of it, but that's what having a place to live is all about. Someone has to do it. I do a few things that aren't on this list as well. And of course, the kids get their share."

1. Sweeping and mopping floors
2. Vacuuming carpets and rugs
3. Dusting surfaces and furniture
4. Cleaning windows and glass surfaces
5. Washing dishes
6. Doing laundry, including folding and putting away clothes
7. Making beds
8. Taking out the trash and recycling
9. Cleaning and disinfecting bathroom fixtures
10. Scrubbing and cleaning toilets
11. Wiping down kitchen countertops and appliances
12. Organizing and decluttering living spaces
13. Watering indoor and outdoor plants
14. Cleaning and disinfecting kitchen sinks
15. Wiping down light switches and doorknobs
16. Sweeping and tidying outdoor areas, such as patios or decks
17. Raking leaves and maintaining the yard
18. Cleaning out the refrigerator and discarding expired items
19. Changing bed linens
20. Cleaning and organizing closets
21. Polishing furniture
22. Disinfecting commonly touched surfaces, such as remote controls and phones
23. Cleaning out and organizing storage spaces, like the attic or garage
24. Wiping down kitchen appliances, like the microwave and oven
25. Cleaning out gutters
26. Dusting and cleaning ceiling fans and light fixtures
27. Washing and cleaning interior and exterior doors
28. Replacing air filters in HVAC systems
29. Testing and replacing batteries in smoke detectors
30. Sweeping and hosing down outdoor walkways and driveways.
31. Cleaning and sanitizing trash bins
32. Vacuuming upholstery and furniture
33. Cleaning and organizing the pantry
34. Defrosting and cleaning the freezer
35. Disinfecting computer keyboards and screens
36. Cleaning and organizing the home office space
37. Cleaning and oiling wooden furniture
38. Wiping down and disinfecting children's toys
39. Checking and replacing light bulbs
40. Cleaning and maintaining household appliances, like the dishwasher and washing machine

"Can we combine a few things as part of the same job?" Francis asked.

"You can do what you want," I answered. "The key issue is deciding together how things will work. You can put some of these in a monthly chore box, or a quarterly chore box, or an as needed box. Make it work for you but do it in a way that is going to move you closer together, rather than pull you apart."

"Is that it, then?" Nyota asked.

"One more thing. I'd like the two of you to watch Andy Stanley's YouTube video series called 'What Happy Couples Know.' In the first video, he talks about how we come into a marriage relationship with a box of hopes, dreams, and desires. We have hopes, dreams, and desires for how many kids we're going to have, for what kind of place we'll live in, for where we'll travel, and even for what kind of chores we'll have to do. These hopes, dreams, and desires might come from the family we grew up in, from what we've seen happening in other families, or just from our own sense of what should be. The problem comes when we say 'I do,' and then hand the box of hopes, dreams, and desires to our spouse for them to fulfill. To our partner, those hopes, dreams, and desires become a box of expectations. All four videos have something important to say."

"We're still reading the *Created for Connection* book by Sue Johnson," Nyota said. "Actually, I'm reading it and summarizing it for Francis. There's a lot of good wisdom in there as well."

"Tim Keller's work, *The Meaning of Marriage,* as well as Gary Thomas's *Sacred Marriage* are also worth some time," I said.

"I notice we didn't finish all the questions," Francis said.

"Why don't you read off the ones that are left? You can do those on your next walk if you want."

Francis lifted his paper.

- What need have you been hesitant to acknowledge with me recently?
- What do you feel worried, nervous, or scared about right now in our relationship?

- When have you been feeling the most turned on?
- How can I best support you right now?
- How can I make your life more wonderful?
- Do you sense we could use more healthy space or closeness right now?

"Yes, I think we'll save those for a walk," Nyota said. "What about the statements on the back?'

"Why don't you read those? They are ideas for things to share with your beloved."

- I appreciate you for...
- I realize I've been negatively impacting our relationship when I...
- I've been feeling guilty or embarrassed about...
- I wish I would do more of...
- I apologize for...
- I've been craving more...
- I want to grow personally by...
- I want to grow together in these ways...
- It sounds really fun to...[69]

FAMILY AND INFIDELITY

"Love at first sight is easy to understand; it's when two people have been looking at each other for a lifetime that it becomes a miracle."[70]— Sam Levenson

Jim and Sharon postponed their session twice before showing up. "Lots happening in the family," Sharon said as she hung her jacket on my new olive wood coat stand. "Nice grain on that," she added.

"Thank you," I said. "Are you sure something else isn't bothering you?"

Jim seemed to freeze in place at the coat stand, keeping his back toward me. Sharon glanced his way and then shrugged. "Do you remember the argument we were having before we first came to you?" she asked. "About the scheduling fiasco, and how I accused Jim of being manipulative and unfaithful?"

"I'm aware of it," I said. "Do you have something more to add?"

She brushed her hair back behind her ears and glanced toward Jim again. He shuffled toward the loveseat where she sat. "It seems that we've both been unfaithful in our own way," she said. "I'll start with me, and Jim can tell you about himself."

"Whenever you're ready," I said.

"With Jim so busy and all, I've been going for coffee with one of the single dads after dropping our kids off at school. It's only been conversations about our kids—and life—and I never thought anything about it. His oldest daughter had a play date at our house on the weekend and said out loud that her dad really enjoyed our coffee times. Jim heard and, of course, got jealous. It wasn't a pretty sight in front of the kids."

I looked toward Jim, who was biting his lip. "I couldn't believe Sharon would do something like that behind my back, but as I was ripping her apart, the thought came to mind that I did that all the time with women from the church and thought nothing of it. Until now, I never stopped to think how it looked to others who saw me. I've been fighting all week with the guilt and shame that I might be unfaithful."

"For Jim, I think this was worse because he had a fling early in our marriage with an old girlfriend and promised me nothing like that would happen again. We rebuilt our trust, but we can't figure out what went wrong this time."

I took out my binder and removed a handout. "Many couples believe that if they can understand the *why*, then they can prevent affairs from happening again."

"But this isn't an affair, is it?" Sharon asked.

"That's something you'll have to talk through," I said. "Sometimes an emotional connection with someone outside the marriage is as shattering as a physical one." I slid a page across to each of them. "Usually, there are several things that combine to stimulate a disconnection with one relationship and a connection with another. What you want to do is recommit to the road of healing and growth in your marriage."

"This looks like it's mainly for people who are physically unfaithful," Jim said.

"True," I said. "It seems you've been there. The shadows of emotional affairs can be long, so interpret each question to apply to your reality. Why don't we read through the statements and check off the ones that apply to your situation—whether we're focusing on a physical or emotional affair?"

- Natural feelings of sexual attraction overwhelmed the prefrontal cortex's ability to reason and were impulsively acted on when the rational brain was impaired.
- I got addicted to the chemical/hormonal rush of emotional connection and/or sex with a novel partner.
- Attention from somebody else boosted self-esteem in a way that was intoxicating.

"These all sound like excuses for making poor choices," Jim said.

"They're showing us that there is much more happening in our bodies, brains, and minds than we realize when we make those poor choices," I said. "It doesn't excuse us, but it might give our partner some room for grace and understanding as we try to reconnect and heal. Let's look at the next options. When there are unresolved childhood wounds like neglect or abuse, perhaps our minds tell us something like:"

- I had affairs to protect myself from feeling dependent on others.
- I was dominated by my parents, and I used my affairs as a way to claim my freedom.
- My parents had affairs, and it taught me to lie and manipulate to get what I want.
- I was indulged as a child, which gave me a warped sense of privilege to have an affair.
- I had an affair to prove I am worthy of love and attention.

"I don't like what this is doing," Sharon said. "Yes, some of this stuff kind of happened in my extended family, but it doesn't excuse it.

The way I grew up doesn't change my responsibility to be faithful to my husband."

"I think this is so sensitive because of all the high-powered leaders who have been caught in adultery," Jim said. "I shudder to think that I might be put in the same category. Their congregations and organizations were shattered when things came into the light."

"Can you imagine the impact and humiliation on their families?" Sharon added. "Our kids would be devastated if we were labeled as unfaithful."

"Before we shelter ourselves too much from all this, there are a few more options on the sheet to look through."

- Emotional connection from somebody else met a need not being met in current relationship.
- Person has had beliefs about infidelity that unfairly justified actions (everybody cheats; what they don't know won't hurt them; I'm staying for my kids; my needs are unmet).
- Person acted out of anger, resentment, or revenge toward partner.
- Person acted in order to reconnect to a part of their identity that has been lost in current relationship or life (free-spirited, powerful, beautiful, caring, understanding).

"This is getting into what you were saying," Sharon said. "Emotional connections and motives are a big part of all this. I admit I did like the attention and affirmation from the man who took me out to coffee. Jim never seemed to have time to listen to me, and he never went out of his way to buy me a muffin, even though I said how much I loved them."

"And I can see how all these women wanting to share their deepest pains made me feel like a caring shepherd," Jim said. "It kind of reminds me of my days in football when all the girls wanted to spend time celebrating with me. I guess it makes me feel like I'm a somebody and that someone wants to hear what I have to say."

"Let's finish the list," I said. "Just check off the ones that apply, and you can talk them through at home later."

- The fantasy world of the affair became an escape from pressures and stressors of life (finances, work, family, illness, loss, etc.).
- Person sought comfort and support from someone outside the relationship.
- Unfair blaming of relationship problems on partner motivated and justified affair.
- Proximity to and much time spent with affair person slowly built connection and/or attraction.
- Shared nonsexual interest or passion with somebody else became sexual (work collaboration, project, hobby).
- Boredom and stagnancy in life
- The opportunity presented itself (someone unexpectedly came onto me, and I got caught up in the moment).
- Unconscious way to exit the relationship
- Possible sex addiction
- Possible porn addiction that created warped sense of reality
- Lack of conscientiousness (selfish, indulgent, can easily lie in order to get what they want, lack of consideration for others)
- Narcissist/sociopathic tendencies
- Being under the influence of a substance
- Unmet needs (physical or emotional) in relationship went unexpressed to partner.
- Unmet needs (physical or emotional) in relationship were regularly expressed and not met.
- Significant life event (death of a loved one, illness, accident, unemployment, life transition, pregnancy, birth of a child, child leaving for college, retirement, etc.).

"That's quite the list," Jim said. "I think a lot of the women I deal with are accusing their husbands of these kinds of things."

"Does that make you more cautious about your own vulnerability to a needy person wanting to take your time and attention?" I asked.

"I think he needs these women," Sharon said. "It's like he's addicted to the attention and affirmation."

"It's not that bad," Jim said. "Someone has to help hurting people."

"When I look at this list, I see him dipping in and out of emotional affairs over and over. It's impacted our marriage more than we've been admitting."

"Don't exaggerate my problems, now that we know you have your own," Jim said.

"What you are involved in almost looks like an addiction cycle."[71] I passed Jim a handout. "Does this make sense? You get emotionally triggered, which opens up a craving for what you want or need. You go to your ritual habit to fill that void, engage in it, and then get swallowed up by guilt and shame."

Jim shook his head vigorously. "I am not addicted. I hate addicts."

"But you're admitting that you have a need to be needed, and that these women you take out to coffee over and over somehow fill that need. Look at the cycle of addiction and imagine you are approached by a woman in need. She triggers your need to be needed, you engage in the ritual of taking her out for coffee, you do it repeatedly, and then you feel guilt and shame when she becomes overly dependent, thus taking time away from your wife and family."

"Yikes!" Jim said. "Now you're saying that not only am I unfaithful, but I'm also an addict?"

"I'm actually saying that before we start judging and labeling each other, it is wise to realize how vulnerable and needy for grace we are. This might be a good time to start renewing, rebuilding, and recommitting yourselves to your own marriage relationship so there are no more regrets. Why don't you spend this week setting up a pathway to connect more purposefully with each other instead of with others outside the relationship? Let me give you one more handout to work with."

"Haven't you given us enough?" Jim asked.

"This sheet is on how to rebuild after an affair. As long as you're honest, vulnerable, and committed, this will be helpful. The acronym used is *REBUILD*."

- *R* means to take responsibility and express remorse.
- *E* means to express empathy toward your hurting partner.
- *B* is to build trust through intentional bonding actions.
- *U* is to understand together why and how it happened so you can prevent a repeat.
- *I* is to invest in the relationship and reprioritize it.
- *L* is to learn to love each other in fulfilling ways again.
- *D* is to design a thriving relationship moving forward from here.

"I've included instructions on how to implement each of these rebuilding steps," I said. "Don't forget to pray a lot together. And be sure to book a few coffee dates with each other, instead of with outsiders."

FAMILY AND CULTURE

Gerhard and Isabella stood outside my office in a heated discussion. They were using German, Portuguese, Swahili, and a smattering of English. The intensity of the interchange is all that alerted me to the significance of their dialogue. I stood in the doorway until Gerhard noticed me and signaled with his eyes to Isabella. She stopped midsentence and brushed past me.

"I wish you knew German," she said in English. "Someone needs to talk sense into this man."

Gerhard followed her to the loveseat, looked around at the other seating options, and finally settled into place beside his wife. "It's all a misunderstanding," he said. "Sometimes culture clashes block our communication."

"That can happen," I said. "Culture is one of the big barriers to communication, but it can also add a lot of spice to our love lives." Neither one of them smiled, so I continued. "You realize by now that your two cultures have different levels of directness and explicitness. You have differing nonverbal cues; you use body language differently. Your humor is different."

"And some cultures have no humor," Isabella said.

Gerhard cleared his throat, drawing attention to his desire to speak. I nodded in his direction and waited.

"Here's a cultural issue," he said. "When it was time to come to this appointment, I told Isabella we needed to leave at 9:15. She agreed, so at 9:15 I am in the car with the engine running waiting to leave. She looks at the clock and begins to get ready to go, so we end up five minutes late."

"That is definitely a cultural issue," I said. "But it could also be a matter of personal interpretation. Did you talk about how she understood your communication?"

"We probably need a referee," he said, turning to his wife. "Isabella, why are you never ready to leave on time when you have agreed to leave on time?"

Instead of looking at him, she turned to me. "This is when I call him German Gerhard. He grew up with an addiction to the clock and to precision, and he can't let go of it." She turned back to her husband. "Dear Gerhard, I know we have had this discussion many times before. When you tell me that we are leaving at 9:15, I understand you to mean that we will begin to leave. I put on my coat and shoes, go to the bathroom, and then I leave. I know you think you're telling me that we are pulling out of the driveway at 9:15, but if you want to do that, then you need to ask me to be ready by 9:10."

"Do you see?" Gerhard said to me. "She twists everything into a cultural conflict."

I leaned toward him. "Can you love her enough to reinterpret what she is saying and accommodate to her style? You've both spent your lives translating Scripture for other people. Can you translate this one simple thing for your best friend?"

Gerhard crossed his arms and leaned back into the loveseat. "It's highly irregular, but I can probably do this one thing."

"There may be other cultural issues for you to think through, since we're on this topic," I said. "How have the dynamics of your birth families impacted the way you do marriage or parenting? For example, have you noticed expectations around how much they want to be involved in your life, or how much they expect you to be involved in theirs?"

Isabella chuckled. "Oh yes, we've noticed. My parents would want us there all the time. Fortunately, our time in Congo has weaned them off too much disappointment. Gerhard's mother wants him to bring the grandchildren over to Germany. I don't think she cares whether I come or not."

"That's not really fair," Gerhard said. "My family hasn't really had the chance to get to know you, and it would be awkward for you since you aren't really fluent in German." He put an arm around his wife and gave a squeeze. "Don't forget, I'm the oldest son, and I do have some responsibility to watch over the family."

"I don't think they trust me yet," Isabella responded. "I was raised Catholic, and Gerhard was raised Lutheran. The way we practice faith together in our family is no problem, but when we visit each other's family, our kids don't know how to worship in those spaces, and our families blame our spouses for warping our children. It gets awkward because we tend to visit during the holidays when the churches are having all their special rituals."

"Have you learned to have discussions with each other around how to navigate those times?"

"Mostly, we just go through it," Isabella said. "We both had to adapt to Congo without knowing anything about that country ahead of time. At least when we visit each other's family homes, one of us knows how to coach the other."

"How do your birth family values impact your decisions?"

"Why do you think we moved to this country?" Gerhard said. "It was easier for our kids to live in a neutral space where they could get a good education, enjoy sports, and build friendships with others from all over the world. It was easier for them, and for us, to be accepted and belong here than in our home countries." He stroked the back of Isabella's hair, and she leaned into him. "My parents wanted me to have the children in a good German university so they could become doctors or engineers. Isabella's family wanted us to move there so the children could find a Latin partner, eat good food, and learn to dance."

"I can agree with them about the food," Isabella said. "It's hard to duplicate a great Latin meal here. You might get something tasty, but you don't quite get the culture, the warmth of the sun, the laughter of the community, the colors in the clothing, or the music of the extended family dropping by unannounced."

Gerhard nodded. "I've only been twice to see her family in Brazil, but the culture there is a lot closer to being in the Congo than Germany's is. I think the children have been spoiled here with all the fast food."

"I think one thing that still takes getting used to is the way we make decisions," Isabella said. "I'm used to having the whole family make decisions together. Everyone knows everyone else's business, and we all have a say. In Gerhard's family, it's every person for themselves, so you never know what anyone else is thinking."

"The only thing you need to worry about is what I'm thinking," Gerhard said. "The way your family has to be in on everything is another good reason I'm glad we're away from all that."

"What's it been like parenting with two such different cultures?" I asked.

"Oh my goodness," Isabella said. "In my culture, children are free to play and enjoy being young. In Gerhard's family, by the time you're six, they're already preparing you for university and a profession. There's no room to grow up. As far as I'm concerned, he's too strict and hard on the boys. We're always sorting out the right way to encourage and support."

"How do you manage conflict?"

"You saw our personality tests," Isabella said. "Do you have copies? Maybe you can read them for us and remind us of who we are."

I took out the profiles and scanned them quickly before reading.

"Gerhard and Isabella test out as ESTP (Doer) and INFP (Mediator). Gerhard is an extreme realist who values action and experience at a high pace. He loves challenges and has an eye for opportunity, especially if it involves a physical experience. He and Isabella had an instant connection when they met because of their passion for life. However, Isabella was a dreamer and an idealist who would rather talk about fascinating ideas and the emotions they generated for her. Excellent listening skills made her a great partner, and she was drawn toward Gerhard's strong values and convictions. But she felt confused with Gerhard's short listening span and his zest to put ideas into life before she had talked them through. Isabella saw her husband as shallow, while Gerhard considered his wife too sensitive and abstract. They focused on their cultural differences as the likely issue.

"How do we work through conflicts with these types? Both Gerhard and Isabella need to bring their divergent strengths into the open rather than seeing them as defects. While they should examine the cultural differences, spending time on a walk discussing appreciation for imagination and creativity for half the time, and then appreciation for practicality and realism for the other half, would build a stronger foundation for harmony. Since both partners value autonomy, this should be worked into the regular calendar while also adding mutually enjoyed experiences. Review your shared values and discover activities that bring those out. Avoid pejorative labels and learn to intentionally point out the positives you see each day."

"I think that about says it all," Isabella said. "I think it's time for another walk."

QUAGMIRE FIVE

Intimacy

"A good marriage is one which
allows for change and growth in
the individuals and in the way they
express their love."
— Pearl S. Buck

When ministry and marriage collide, the result often shows up in
the area of intimacy. This issue is far more than what happens
between the sheets, although its impact can definitely be felt there. Intimacy is impacted by busyness, the filling of our love accounts, the rituals
we establish and practice, the depth of our emotional connection, the
fears that paralyze us, the heart listening we practice regularly, the brakes
and accelerators we learn with our libidos, and the past abuses or addictions that rise under tension. Seasoned leaders are likely familiar with the
apostle Paul's instruction in 1 Corinthians:

> Since sexual immorality is occurring, each man should
> have sexual relations with his own wife, and each woman with her own husband. The husband should fulfill
> his marital duty to his wife, and likewise the wife to
> her husband. The wife does not have authority over
> her own body but yields it to her husband. In the same
> way, the husband does not have authority over his own
> body but yields it to his wife. Do not deprive each other except perhaps by mutual consent and for a time, so

that you may devote yourselves to prayer. Then come together again so that Satan will not tempt you because of your lack of self-control. (1 Corinthians 7:2-5)

Knowing this, and practicing it, can make all the difference in mitigating collisions around intimacy. The issue to recognize is that our covenant is as crucial as our commission while we live out the symbolism of the marriage relationship.

INTIMACY AND BUSYNESS

"It isn't much good having anything exciting, if you can't share it with somebody." —Winnie the Pooh

Francis and Nyota showed up with the specific desire to address the gap of intimacy they felt in their relationship. Their busyness after a dozen years of supporting different social causes; their hidden addictions to technology; and their quest to help numerous outside relationships meant that their schedule had no margin for alone time. This is one area most leaders shy away from. After all, if you've had children, you must have figured this out somewhere along the way.

We started with the basics. "Most relationships are founded on trust," I said. "How would you measure your level of trust at this point?"

Nyota waved her hand. "Considering that Francis immediately assumed I was off having an affair while he was at his conference, I don't think we're too high on that scale."

Francis winced. "I didn't exactly assume you were having an affair. I just didn't know where you were. I came home convicted that we needed to do something to improve our relationship, but you were nowhere to be found. And there was no note explaining how to contact you."

Nyota glared at him. "So, your idea of solving our intimacy issues was to leave a message on my phone saying, 'Where are you?'"

Francis looked down and twirled his thumbs. "I probably could have handled that better. At least we're here."

"Have you ever heard of the concept of love tanks?" I asked.

"I think we heard about those in our premarital counseling," Francis said.

"Just as a review, a love tank is an imaginary tank that lets us know how loved we're feeling. It relies on other people to keep it filled. You can put holes in it and empty it through things like criticism, contempt, defensiveness, and stonewalling. Dr. John Gottman calls these the four horsemen of a relationship apocalypse."[72]

"Criticism sure does a number on me," Francis said.

"And your defensiveness does a number on me," Nyota added.

"So, we are in agreement," I said. "Criticism is different than a critique or complaint. When you attack your partner's character, you are attacking their core identity. A complaint might sound like 'Hon, I was scared when I came home, and you weren't here. I thought we had agreed to leave notes or texts for each other if we were heading out.' A criticism might focus on how selfish or thoughtless your partner is. Do you see the difference?"

"If this is a critique of how we've been communicating, I get it," Francis said.

"Contempt is another level, one where we actually get mean," I said. "This is where disrespect, mocking, sarcasm, name-calling, eye-rolling, and scoffing would come in. Here, you want the other person to feel despised and worthless. You are taking a position of moral superiority. This is fueled by negative thinking and can result in poor health for your partner if you keep it up."

Nyota scooted forward in her chair and glanced at Francis. "You better not blame me for that flu you caught. We're not that far gone."

"That's good," I said, "because habitual contempt is the greatest predictor of a relationship breaking down beyond repair."

"What about my defensiveness?" Francis asked.

"This is the usual response to criticism," I answered. "You might play the innocent victim, make excuses, and act to make your partner back off. It's easy to not only make excuses for yourself but to try to redirect the blame onto your partner. Taking responsibility is key to recovering some healthy communication and connection."

"I don't think either of us use stonewalling," Nyota said. "We usually communicate one way or another. We just never get beyond the surface to the intimate."

"There are antidotes to embrace," I said. "We'll look at those sometime if we see that criticism, contempt, defensiveness, or stonewalling get in the way. In the meantime, let's get back to our love languages." I laid out a set of handouts in front of them. "When's the last time you figured out your love languages?"

"I've heard of them," Nyota said. "Something about touch and time. My friends seem to have theirs all worked out."

"Since you two are techies, why don't you go to quiz@5lovelanguages.com/quizzes/couples-quiz/ and take the test? Find your results and fill out this sheet." I pointed to the place where scores could be entered into the five boxes.

	Partner A	Partner B
Acts of Service		
Gifts		
Quality Time		
Touch		
Words of Affirmation		

"Since we all give and receive love differently, it might be helpful to know how you can best share love in a way that's understood as such. The test measures whether you give and receive love primarily through touch, gifts, quality time, acts of service, or words of affirmation. You might think you're expressing love in the way you understand it, but it might not be getting through to your partner."

While the two of them worked through the test, I stared out the window at torrents of rain blocking the horizon. I hoped the weather was no indication of how things would progress here inside with this couple.

Nyota finished first and slid her paper across my desk. "No surprises for me," she said.

When Francis finished his quiz, he jotted down his scores and clutched the paper to his chest. "Am I going to get to see Nyota's scores?"

"Of course," I said. "Why don't you lay your papers side by side and see what you've come up with?" I took a third sheet and filled it in with both scores.

The sheets were telling.

	Partner A Nyota	Partner B Francis
Acts of Service	1	5
Gifts	2	4
Quality Time	3	2
Touch	5	3
Words of Affirmation	4	1

"What do you understand about yourselves from seeing these results side by side?" I asked.

Nyota looked up first, so I nodded toward her. "Francis wants me to tell him how wonderful he is all the time, and I expect him to do something to get the appreciation he wants."

Francis turned toward her. "I tell you all the time how much I appreciate you doing the gardens, the laundry, the cleaning, the meals. I even tell you I love you for what you do."

Nyota faced him. "You're missing the point. When my love language is acts of service, it means I want you helping me with the gardens, the laundry, and the cleaning. Maybe not the meals."

"So, Francis, summarize these charts for me," I said.

He scanned the paper in front of us. "Nyota's top love language is acts of service, which means that when she does stuff around the house, she thinks she's telling me that she loves me. For me, chores are work, so it doesn't speak to me in any form. My number one language is words of affirmation, which means I want some verbal appreciation for just showing up, whereas she doesn't care a whole lot about how many things I tell her I appreciate."

"None of our love languages are lining up," Nyota said. "He won't do anything, he won't give me anything, and all he wants is my time, affirmation, and touch."

"I think both of you know that it takes sacrifice to make love work," I said. "The language you identify with comes naturally, so you don't have to work on that a whole lot. You do, however, have to figure out how you're going to speak your partner's love language in a way that hits them in the heart. You also need to step away from your technology enough to put it into action. That's your homework this week. Take time each day to speak each other's language enough that your partner feels it deeply. You'll notice the difference when their love tank starts filling up."

INTIMACY AND THE LOVE ACCOUNT

> **"Love at first sight is easy to understand; it's when two people have been looking at each other for a lifetime that it becomes a miracle."[73]** — **Sam Levenson**

Gerhard and Isabella had already wrestled through their love language issues but still felt that their love tanks were too dry. Between their clashes over culture, her feeling of being trapped, and their lack of positive childhood environments, they were in a state of relational paralysis. On one hand, they were trying to top up their love tanks; on the other, they were poking holes in the base of their tanks and undoing any good they had accomplished.

This time I had a PowerPoint slide showing on my laptop.

"Here you can see Dr. John Gottman's magic ratio for a happy relationship: at least five positive interactions for every one negative interaction. The closer a couple is to reaching the 20:1 ratio, the happier they will be." I flipped a page and drew a couple of columns on the back. "This is what he says is needed for a stable, healthy, and happy relationship. We talked about love tanks. Think of this as a love account. You're making deposits and withdrawals. When your love account is full, then connection, joy, togetherness, resilience, and even intimacy will take care of themselves. If your account is low, then don't expect much in the way of spice or zip in your marriage."

"So, it's okay if we have some negative confrontation to sort out our issues, but we need a lot of positive vibes to get to the making up," Isabella said.

I nodded. "It's inevitable that some conflict will arise, and that keeps you alert and aware. You just can't stay in the negative side of things for too long if you want to move ahead. With a formula of 20:1, you'll be very happy. With a 5:1 ratio, you'll be moderately happy. Less than that and there will be conflict, tension, and breakdown in the relationship."

"So, how do we do this thing when it's not in our nature or culture?" Gerhard asked.

"I'm sure that in your cultures, there are times when you express appreciation for something special—maybe a gift at Christmas or a special meal or event. Most of that can be done from our heads and never reach our hearts. It's what comes from the heart that connects us to each other."

"I've been telling him that for years," Isabella said. "Sometimes I think my culture got all the heart, and his got all the head."

"You actually can wire your brain through your heart," I said. "If you can learn the art of meaningful appreciation, you will learn how inspiring and motivating this all is."

"Okay, what do we do?" Gerhard asked.

"You get specific, personal, and complimentary."

"Do you have an example?" Isabella asked.

"Sure, here's one. Isabella, thank you for coming on time today. It is so encouraging to see you smiling and prepared, and it makes me feel like what we do here is something special. I leave here at the end of the day feeling like what we've accomplished is really going to have lasting change, not just for today but maybe for a lifetime."

There was a moment of silence before Gerhard stepped in. "Do you expect me to go through all that every time she does the dishes, or vacuums, or bakes cookies?"

"Aren't you the one who wanted to know how to fill your wife's love tank?"

"Yes, but she doesn't even care about all that. She wants something genuine."

I smiled. "Exactly. You have to express genuine thanks. Let her know how what she did made you feel, why you appreciated it, and how it has benefited and improved your life."

"For a cookie?"

"No, for her love tank."

"Do you have anything else?" Isabella asked.

"How about Date Night Discovery Cards?"[74]

"Is this more love tank stuff?" Gerhard asked.

"No, it's intimacy stuff," I said.

"What's it about?" he asked. "What do I have to do?"

"You don't *have* to do anything," I said. "You *get* to help your wife bloom like a flower and then enjoy the aroma of her love in bloom."

"You better explain it," Isabella said. "He'll listen better to you."

I picked up a stack of double-sided cards and put them face down in front of us. "Okay, we're going to play for practice," I said. "Rather, you're going to play with each other, and I'll coach you from the sidelines. You'll pick up a card and read the open-ended question. Your partner will respond, and you can only give positive feedback on what they answer. Let go of all your distractions and just enjoy. There should be no one-word answers."

"Okay, let's do this," Isabella said.

"You first," Gerhard said. "I'll pick a card and ask you the question." He drew a card. "How are you feeling about your work these days?"

Isabella smiled. "Thank you for asking. You've never asked that question of me before. I love translating the book of Mark. It's so straightforward and clear. Jesus seems so real. I'm excited with the challenge of finding just the right word to get the fullest meaning across. I love how it sounds in my ear and how it rolls off my tongue. It makes me want to do a dance of joy with the children. Especially Carlos. Do you notice how he loves music and moves across the floor? I love working with the children even more than I love translating. Each of them brings their own energy and challenge into our lives. Did you notice how they look at you while you're reading the devotions each night?"

"Wait a minute!" Gerhard said. "This is about you. Do you really have to give such a long answer?"

"Are you genuinely wanting to know me for who I am?" Isabella asked. "If you're honestly curious, then your patience may pay off—I may just want to get to know you as well."

"We call that being curious," I said. "We wonder and look under. We see what is behind the surface of our partner."

"My turn," Isabella said. She snatched up a card. "What adventures would you love to have before you die?"

Gerhard frowned, then straightened, then sank into silence. We all sat for at least a minute until, finally, he smiled. "Kayaking down the Amazon, climbing the Andes, and a safari balloon ride over the Serengeti."

Isabella had her mouth open. "Anything else?" she finally said.

He knit his eyebrows together and then relaxed. "An Alaskan cruise, a night in Tokyo, an Olympic hockey game, a trip to the Holy Land, and a look at the pyramids of Egypt."

"Wow!" Isabella responded. "Why haven't you said anything about all this?"

"Money," he responded.

"But we could view it all onscreen. We could live it through the eyes of others until our own opportunity comes."

"I never thought of that," he said.

"That's why you get to share date night questions," I said. "There's a whole stack of them waiting for those little gaps in your day. You never know what's in the heart of your partner until you open the door with a question."

"And that's intimacy?" Gerhard asked.

"Intimacy is about getting to know the one you love more and more every day. This is one way to open the door for that to happen. Take the cards and practice this week. You may be surprised at what happens when Isabella realizes you really want to know what's under the surface."

Isabella reached for the top button of her blouse with raised eyebrows.

Gerhard straightened, then smiled. "I think I better take those cards and get home," he said.

INTIMACY AND CONNECTION RITUALS

"If your partner is complaining that you seem more focused on your social media profile than your marital status, that's an issue you need to take seriously, even if you disagree." — John Gottman

Hailey and Simon got their holiday in. Despite this, due to an intense flurry of interaction and calls with desperate youth, their time away was awkward.. They both continued to text and respond to the youths they'd left behind.

"We unpacked at the chalet, and it was like we didn't know what to do next," Hailey said. "We went for a walk, and that gave us a good chance to talk, but it was like we'd lost our rhythm and sense of comfort with each other. The holiday almost seemed like a waste of money."

"I think it became clear that we've lost our zip," Simon said. "We haven't had our regular interactions—we got too busy—and so it's not surprising. We're both counselors and know what we have to do. It seems we just need some coaching to get us back in sync."

"As people who work with people, you understand how much our mindset matters," I said. "You know the importance of giving honor and respect to someone you love. Honoring means that you regard the other with admiration, you give special recognition to them, and you fulfill your promises to them."

"I'm thinking that goes both ways," Hailey said. "It can't be only the woman who has to kowtow to her husband."

"Sounds like this is a sensitive issue," I said. Simon frowned from his space, but I continued. "The mindset we bring to relationship matters. As we grow in our relationship, we develop belief systems about each other, and this influences how we treat and respond to the other person. If our mind is fixed that our partner won't change, or if we've fixated on some form of what "ideal" looks like in our relationship, then we can get stuck right where you are. If you choose a growth mindset, you'll soon realize that work, time, practice, and focus, can help you develop the needed skills to move on from here."

"You're saying we can't live with assumptions about each other," Simon said. "We can't read each other's minds, and we have to actually communicate what we think and feel."

"We know this," Hailey said. "It's just doing it in the heat of the moment that's the issue."

"The key is to consistently choose the growth mindset ahead of time so it becomes your reflex response in the heat of the moment. Thoughts are powerful informers, and they erupt from our core beliefs and stimulate our behaviors. Managing your feelings is crucial, as you both know."

"Of course, our internal and external boundaries have to be managed as well," Hailey said. "But I can see how my beliefs and feelings about Simon would affect the way I treat him. I do sometimes dismiss what he says or fall into criticizing his ideas. And then I really can't be bothered responding to his desires for intimacy."

"So, how could you adjust to a growth mindset before this kind of thinking gets entrenched? What are some thoughts to build on as you think about your partner?"

"I like to think that we have each other's backs," Simon said.

"I think we both deserve fairness, empathy, and compassion," Hailey added.

"I imagine we need to realize what is ours to control and what isn't," Sam said. "Like, I shouldn't try to manage Hailey's emotions."

Hailey leaned forward. "I think we should invest in each other and maybe even try to celebrate each other's successes."

"I think you have it," I said. "Frustration, anger, and unforgiveness lay a foundation for rigid and critical beliefs about our partner. When you start saying 'you never' or 'you always,' you're moving toward a fixed mindset. Even a small adjustment like 'I notice you often' or 'I wonder why you so often…' can help."

"We still have to be honest," Hailey said. "Simon has to manage his own feelings. I'm not holding back what I need to say just because he's stuck with his inner child."

Simon held out his hands. "I think the issue is that we can't only be about saying what we think. There has to be some celebration and affirmation about something, sometime."

"True!" I said. "Your partner needs to know that they deserve your affection, appreciation, or admiration sometimes. Withholding positive support is not moving you toward growth. Happier couples can argue, but they pay strong attention to their positive moments together."

"Maybe we don't have enough of those positive moments," Hailey said.

"Perhaps you need some time to brainstorm some small, medium, and large rituals to act as rails for your love train to run on. It's become clear that your schedule—and the intensity of all those young bodies in crisis—is wreaking havoc on this relationship. We've talked about putting the big rocks into your jar first, before allowing those around you to hand you their rocks. You two are a team, and your commitment to each other is going to guard your times of intimacy."

Simon motioned for attention as I slid another handout toward him. "Is this where you want us to write down things like date nights? You want us to actually schedule our passion times?"

"Is it happening when you don't schedule your passion times?" I asked.

Hailey sighed. "Can you explain what you mean by small, medium and large?"

SMALL	MEDIUM	LARGE
1.	1.	1.
2.	2.	2.
3.	3.	3.
4.	4.	4.
5.	5.	5.

"Okay," I said. "Small rituals are those that usually take from thirty seconds to a couple of hours. It's something you would do each day as a matter of intentional habit. It might include things like a hello or goodbye kiss, a snuggle in the morning, a walk, a greeting hug, or a love note on the counter."

"You're doing the work for us," Simon said. "There's no more room left after we include those."

"Don't include anything you're not willing to follow up on," I said. "And both of you need to agree before you write it down. There may be other original things you want to put in place."

"Are we limited by the number?" Hailey asked. "Why don't we brainstorm in pencil and then finish up writing what we agree to in pen?"

"Whatever works is good by me," Simon said.

I pulled a pencil and a yellow highlighter out of my drawer and put them on the table with the pens. "Just remember, you need to make this a daily thing, so you do only what is going to help you and not become another burden."

I gave them a few minutes as they set their list in place.

"Now, the medium list," I said. "Medium rituals are those that might take an entire evening or an afternoon. Remember, these are alone times that will give you time to build your intimacy, so, yes, a date night would be written down here."

Simon reached for the pencil. "With all the kids around, we'll have to lock ourselves into our room, and then you know what they'll be doing on the outside?"

"I'm leaving it to you to clear the house if you want time alone with me," Hailey said. "I'm not turning our time into a circus act. Are we allowed to say that no phones are allowed in the bedroom?"

"So, you want me to clear the kids out of the house, but you want to restrict our intimacy to the bedroom?" Simon asked.

Hailey blushed. "I know exactly what you're up to. If you want a piece of the pie, you're going to have to warm it up first. I don't do drive-through."

"This is good," I said. "Having a code language to draw each other out shows familiarity and comfort coming back. Keep practicing."

"Let's get the rituals written down so we can put this stuff into action," Simon said.

Hailey picked up the pen. "If I put down in ink 'gym, walk, shower, dinner and date night' as five separate things, you know what I'm saying, right?"

"You're moving from zero to sixty in seconds, girl. Are you sure you want to move that fast after the holiday we just had? Remember, you're saying this is going to be our weekly ritual."

"You afraid to be this close, this often?" Hailey asked.

"I'm just saying, let's save a little for the large rituals. We've got years ahead of us. If we're with each other every day, then going away will leave nothing special on the table."

"Oh, I can think of a few things that might be left on the table," Hailey said. "Okay, what are these big rituals all about?"

I glanced at Simon. He was sitting back, staring at his wife as if he'd never met this side of her. "The large rituals include things that last more than a day. It's the weekend away, the retreat, the camping trip, the vacation—whatever you do on your own over an extended time."

"I'll take all of those," Hailey said. She handed the pen to Simon. "Here! You write it down so that we can see your commitment in your own handwriting." When her husband took the pen, she added, "How are you planning to clear out the kids this evening?"

"You know it's study night," Simon said. "And Jenny is coming for a piano lesson. And I promised Terry he could watch the game tonight."

"Your loss," Hailey said, sitting back.

"Wait a minute," Simon said. "You didn't warn me ahead of time."

Hailey crossed her arms and smiled coyly. "You set the table and I'll feed your hunger, but I'm not going to be an afterthought whenever you have a two-minute break in your day."

Simon fidgeted in his chair and picked up the list again. "It'll take time to call everyone."

"That's up to you," Hailey said. "I'm sure I can get absorbed in Pinterest, Tik Tok, or the shopping channel and forget about everything we've discussed today."

"I think we better pick this up at the next session," Simon said.

"Don't forget your papers," I said. "I'd hate for you to forget your commitments."

Intimacy and Emotional Connections

"Whatever our souls are made of, his and mine are the same." - Emily Brontë, *Wuthering Heights*

Jim and Sharon walked through the door, hand in hand. There was a clear shift in their usual demeanor. I was eager to find out what had changed for them.

"I see you've had a good week," I said.

"Actually, no!" Jim said, flopping down on the loveseat. "We spent most of the week sorting through our poisonous words and asking for forgiveness. We spent a lot of time in our heads and realized that we didn't really know how to connect with our hearts."

"You seem happy," I said.

"Confession and forgiveness make the heart light," Sharon said, spinning and moving to the water cooler. "We saw how often we got stuck in the power struggle area, and we wanted to move toward thriving instead. We tried a few things but thought we should get some help on where to go next."

"Have you thought about what kind of emotional leaks may be draining your love tanks? I asked.

"Define emotional leaks?" Jim said.

"Emotional leaks are activities you use, consciously or unconsciously, to avoid close connection with your spouse. They might even be healthy things like exercise or spending an evening playing games with friends, but they don't give you space to work on your marriage. They can be good, but they can become leaks when the end result is disconnection and separation."

"Like, when I see Susan playing solitaire on her computer, and instead of taking the initiative to give her a cuddle, I flip on the game," Jim said.

"Exactly!"

"Does cuddling the cat instead of cuddling Jim fit in this area?" Susan asked. "Or playing solitaire, or going out with my friends for lunch on Saturdays, when I know Jim will be home?"

"A thing only becomes an emotional leak when it is done consistently and intentionally, to avoid connection. Everything has a time and place. If you become aware of emotional leaks, deal with them one at a time. Be easy on yourself. Trace down when you tend to let that leak take over from your relationship. Are you stressed, fearful, anxious, angry, lonely, or sad? Go for a walk together and talk this through. Write yourself a small contract, stating which leak you are going to stop and what activity you're going to do instead to enhance your relationship."

"Okay, if I only have to shut off one at a time, I might be able to do that," Jim said.

I opened my binder and removed yet another handout. "It sounds like you need to create a safe space for emotional connection. On this page there are numerous statements that will help you move toward the commitment phase. Intimacy is stimulated when there is authenticity, transparency, and open-hearted relationship." I paused a moment for their response, but hearing none, I pressed on. "If there are secrets or lies or withholding in the relationship, it will be toxic to intimacy. Sometimes we don't share our real thoughts and feelings because we're afraid to be ridiculed, shamed, or blamed."

"Or that we'll end up in another conflict," Jim said, looking toward Sharon.

She turned from the water cooler, biting her nail. "You have to understand—I didn't feel this way at work. I was a senior leader, and my staff and volunteers didn't question me or my integrity like my own husband does. My heart feels like it's boxed up and hidden away. Some days I don't want him to come home."

"Sounds like you might not be feeling safe," I said.

Sharon moved toward the love seat, waited for Jim to shift over, and then slumped into place. "Don't get me wrong. I love this guy. But sometimes I get overwhelmed and don't know how to do the heart connection thing. I feel so in control at work and so out of control at home."

"Let's look at these statements," I said, handing another paper to Sharon. "Alternate by reading a phrase and then letting your partner read the next one. Give a moment between each one so we can process what is being said. Sharon, you can start."

Sharon squinted at the sheet and then set her glasses in place. "I commit to seeing you as my teammate and ally." She lowered the sheet and glanced at Jim. "I do want to do that. Sometimes it just feels that you've switched teams on me."

"Let's read the statement and give a minute to process," I said. "Each of these statements might bring up some emotions we need to deal with."

Jim set his jaw and focused on his sheet. "I commit to loving, accepting, and honoring you."

Sharon doffed her shoes and curled her feet up underneath her. "I commit to creating a safe space for your authentic, honest, and transparent voice to be expressed and heard." She pushed her glasses up on her forehead. "Do I get to judge whether his voice is authentic, or do I have to assume it is?"

"Your mindset will make a difference in what happens afterward," I said.

Jim took his turn. "I commit to supporting you in feeling your feelings to completion, without trying to quiet, interrupt, disregard, or invalidate them."

They looked at each other. "That's a big commitment," Sharon said. She scanned her paper. "I commit to receiving your feedback with an open heart and mind, and to embracing a spirit of curiosity and understanding."

"I'd appreciate that," Jim said. "I commit to being completely honest with both of us so that the truth can bring me closer to myself and to you."

"Will these statements apply to both of us, even if we're not the one who's reading them?" Sharon asked.

"Of course," I said.

"I commit to giving you permission to feel and see things differently from me," Jim said.

"I commit to never using this information against you and, instead, using it to support you and our relationship," Sharon added.

"I commit to disabling my defenses and being willing to change and grow so I can be a better, healthier, and happier person and partner," Jim finished.

"Those are big commitments," Sharon observed.

"Your homework is to spend every day this week alternating back and forth in saying these commitments to each other. If you have comments to make to cement them in place, you can discuss it then. For now, I want us to look at three powerful questions that impact emotional intimacy." I handed each of them another handout. "Jim, you will slowly and repeatedly ask Sharon these three questions, one at a time, until you feel she's said everything she needs to say. Then you will thank her and move on. Okay, begin when you are ready."

Jim turned toward Sharon and waited for her gaze to connect. "What do you really want?"

Sharon almost gasped before answering. "I want us to get along," she said.

"What do you really want after that?" Jim asked.

Sharon tugged at her earlobe and sighed. "I want to want to come home."

"And what do you really want after that?"

"I want to feel like I'm wanted and needed."

"And what do you really want after that?"

"I want to curl up in your arms and to feel safe," she said, tears forming in her eyes.

The two of them cuddled together, side by side on the loveseat, Jim gently stroking her hair.

"Powerful stuff," Jim said.

"Ask the second question in the same way," I said.

He glanced at his sheet. "What are you afraid of?"

She quietly rested her head on his shoulder. Finally, she heaved another sigh. "Now? I'm afraid this might be a dream. I'm afraid to go back to work and face budgeting and a staff evaluation. I'm afraid of what the doctor might say to me at my checkup next week. I'm afraid of what is going on with my dad's health. There's a lot I'm afraid of."

"What is your biggest fear right now?" Jim asked.

She straightened and looked deep into his eyes. "I'm afraid that we'll go back to the way we were, that you'll never forgive me, and that I might be successful at work but a failure at home."

"That's big," Jim said. "What is your biggest fear of all those fears?"

She reached for another Kleenex. "I'm afraid that you'll get tired of our fighting and leave me."

"And what's the fear behind that fear?"

Sharon started trembling and finally quieted herself under Jim's gentle stroking. "I'm afraid I'll be all alone."

"I'm here," he said. "I'm here. I'm not going anywhere."

"There's one more question," I said.

"What do you love about me?" Jim asked.

"Now you ask me," Sharon said. "I'd say your omelettes, but I don't think that's the point of this. I think I love your patience with me."

"And what do you love about that patience with you?"

"I love that you usually give me the space to figure things out when stuff goes wrong."

"And what do you love about the fact that I give you space to figure things out?"

"I love that you value what I think and feel, and that you believe in me. That I'll figure things out."

"And what do you love about me because of all that?"

"I love that you're an anchor when it's stormy. That I can rely on you. Trust you."

"That's about it," I said. "Now, you can go home and do the same thing in reverse."

Sharon gave Jim a kiss. "Not sure I need to ask all those questions. I can see the man I married. I think I just need a little cuddle time."

INTIMACY AND FEARS

> **"The heart has its reasons of which reason knows nothing."—Blaise Pascal, "Pensées"**

Esther and Phil came in for their session after a weekend away. Esther paced the room and glanced out the window instead of sitting beside Phil. He slipped off his shoes and settled sideways on the love seat, watching her. After my greeting, I waited for her to join us in our space, but she anchored herself in place.

"I can see that something's going on for the two of you," I said.

"Our time away was a nightmare," Esther said, without looking back at me. "I've never felt so out of control. It felt like I was someone else going through the motions with a stranger. I had panic attacks, crazy thoughts."

Phil turned back toward me. "She was questioning her faith, her marriage covenant— everything we've built our life on."

"I don't know what's wrong with me," Esther said. "He's my husband. We don't get together that often, but it felt like I was afraid of intimacy all weekend, and I didn't know what to do."

"Let's take that seriously," I said. "There are usually one of five fears at work when this happens."

"You mean this happens with others?" Esther said. "I don't know how people function like this."

I slipped two handouts on clipboards to both of them as Esther came over to stand by the desk. "Just to keep this fair, I'll get both of you to take the fear of intimacy assessment. The first sheet has a series of questions, and the second is the score sheet. Take your time answering the thirty questions. You can see that each one is answered with *Always, Usually, Sometimes, Rarely,* or *Never.*"

Esther grabbed another chair and set up at the desk, while Phil stayed in place on the love seat. I flipped through other handouts as Esther and Phil scored out their assessment. When they were done, we copied their scores onto a single sheet and tallied the columns to discover the predominant fear.

"What do you notice?" I asked.

"Fear of abandonment and fear of losing myself are close together at the top," Esther said.

"Fear of being attacked is fairly strong for me, but I'm not fearful about too much," Phil said.

I scanned the results. "This might seem surprising, considering how confident you are in your executive role," I said to Esther. "Those who fear abandonment tend to be a bit clingy and are anxious about being left. You seem fairly independent. Have you ever doubted Phil's commitment to you, or do you find yourself getting jealous about his relationships?"

"Okay, the secret is out of the bag," Esther said. "It drives me crazy to think of him home on his computer all day looking at who knows what. It's easier to stay at work and focus on what I have to do. Some days I come home wondering if he's still going to be there."

"You've never told me any of this," Phil said.

"I didn't want you to think I was too controlling," Esther said. "Or paranoid."

"It would be good for us to look at the issue of secure attachment and the expectations you might have of your partner in meeting your core needs," I said. "My understanding from your love story is that Phil was attracted to you because you displayed so much independence, confidence, and passion."

"Fooled him, didn't I?" Esther said.

"Have you ever felt this sense of abandonment in any of your other relationships?" I asked.

"Only when my parents divorced, when I was in high school," Esther answered. "And when my boyfriend took advantage of me and then ignored me." She got up and moved toward the window again. "I think there were others."

"It may be important for you to deal honestly with some of those core issues you've been hiding," I said. "It's important to come into your relationship whole, healthy, and nourished so that you're not depending on your spouse to meet all your needs."

"If that's the case, he might be waiting a long time," Esther said. "Anyway, it's too late. We're already married and in the middle of this quagmire."

"So, Phil," I said, "to help your beloved with her fear, it would be great if you could assure her that you're not going anywhere. Realize that her responses to you are based on fear and not on whether she loves you or not. Making all those calendar appointments helps her believe that you'll be there for her when she needs you most."

Phil rose and stood beside Esther. "I'm not going anywhere," he said. "I love you for who you are, not for what you do."

Esther tweaked Phil's chin and turned back, sitting on the love seat. "What about the other fear?"

"The fear of losing yourself is about thinking that the relationship is swallowing up your independence, that your partner is trying to control you. It's about feeling trapped or limited in some way."

Esther glanced at Phil and held his gaze. "I don't usually feel that way while I'm working. Only when I'm home, or when there's a conflict with work and family."

"If you're going to get to thriving in your relationship, it's important to learn to lean into your partner for strength, to open yourself up to feedback, to practice flexibility, and to listen carefully to what Phil is saying from his heart."

"I guess I may be afraid that if I give him too much control or influence over me, I'll lose my independence. Some days I feel the only one I can count on is myself."

"You can help your relationship by carefully weighing Phil's requests, and you can say 'yes' as much as possible."

"Are we talking sex?" Esther asked.

"More than that," I said. "You probably know by now what things are important to him. Of course, you have to weigh what's important to you, but be open to what's important to him as well. Nurture your own interests so you feel secure and cared for, but reach toward him in any way you can."

"So, how do I deal with this fear?" Phil asked.

"Good question," I responded. "Esther might step back from you when this fear is strong. You might want to press in on her to comfort her. Be careful of what you ask of her at that moment. Take time for a positive conversation and look for something creative you can both connect over. Allow Esther some freedom, some choice. If you give her space when she needs it, you may find she is able to come closer."

"What about Phil's fear?" Esther asked. "I'm not the only psycho. It's not like I'm attacking him all the time."

"I said that I don't really have that many fears," Phil said. "But sometimes, I'm not sure what you'll say, and I get a little sensitive at those times."

I rose to stand with them. "Phil, you may just need to be careful about what you share at times. You can't let yourself sink into looking for ulterior motives in what your wife is saying when she is kind. You could look back at your past relationships to see if there are roots you might need to deal with. You're responsible to protect yourself when you feel vulnerable, so don't ever start blaming Esther for what is going on inside you."

"Any tips for me on that one?" Esther said.

"Be positive, warm, encouraging, affirming, appreciative, and kind as much as possible. Avoid criticizing, teasing, sarcasm, blaming, or condescension. Take some deep breaths and give yourself space when you catch yourself crossing the line on this. Watch your words, your tone of voice, and your body language."

"Wow!" Jim said. "I can see how fear gets in the way of intimacy. It really doesn't matter how long we've been married; if we haven't dealt with these giants under the surface, we'll wander around a wilderness for the rest of our lives."

"Schedule safe time for each other, get some help to dig up the roots of those fears, and be gentle as you come together. Take it slow. Be there. We're here to walk each other home."

INTIMACY AND HEART LISTENING

> **"Sometimes we don't know what is so painful to us in a particular event until we can really explore it with our partner. And sometimes it is very hard to just come out and show the core of our hurt to the one who hurt us. But the pain always makes sense if we relate it to our attachment needs and fears."**
> **—Sue Johnson**

Sam and Hannah chose to check in through Zoom when we reached the issue of intimacy. Hannah was still holed up in her own place and sorting through what she wanted out of the relationship. She opened up her link but left a photo of herself on the screen instead of turning on her camera. Sam was lounging in his media room, with a football game clearly visible on the television in the background.

"Welcome, both of you," I began. "I know we agreed to talk through the importance of brakes and accelerators for intimacy, but since you're still separated, I wonder if we could focus on heart listening."

"Fine by me," Sam said. "You better check with Hannah. She's the one who won't let me near her."

Hannah's voice came through clearly. "If it's about you listening better, then I'm good with that. I can see you have the game on, so how's that going to help? You're always focused on something or someone else."

The television screen on Sam's monitor went dark, and he adjusted the camera angle on his laptop.

"Okay, then," I said. "It seems like our defenses are up fairly high, and this is to help ease things so we can actually hear what's going on for our partner. I'm going to share my screen and let you see an anacronym which explains what heart listening is all about. Sam, will you read what you see?"

His voice came through loud and clear.

H *Hear* your beloved by reflecting the essence of what they said.

E Offer *empathy*. Imagine what it is like to really feel what they are feeling.

A Find things to *appreciate* about them regarding what they shared.

R *Relax* into your heart. Take some deep breaths.

T Come with a spirit of *togetherness* and *teamwork*.

"Any comments?" I asked.

"Seems like a formula," Hannah said. "I can't imagine how talking like a robot is going to help me feel close to anyone, especially Sam."

"It's a process that takes practice," I said. "When you learned to drive, or to play the piano, you had to think through everything you did. When you learned a computer program, you had to focus on the next steps. When you took courses in university, you had to learn the basics before you felt comfortable enough to do what you needed to do without too much conscious thought."

"Makes sense to me," Sam said. "If what we're doing now isn't working, then we need to try something different. There's a lot of chaos in my thoughts and emotions before we even get to some serious dialogue. I can choose to empathize with and appreciate my wife."

"Yeah, now that I'm gone," Hannah said. "You should have tried this earlier. If you want intimate connection, there's a lot of work left for you to do."

"Feeling heard is a great place to start," I said. "Our defenses can really get in the way when our partner opens up our raw spots and spins us into our fear dance. Taking a deep breath and trying to see what's behind someone's words can help soften the conversation and open the heart for something deeper."

Sam disappeared from view but returned in a moment with a mug of coffee. "What are you saying? Sometimes I think we might be sharing the same space but talking in monologues into the air."

"Let's actually try to practice this exercise," I said. "Hannah, you tell Sam what's on your mind, and Sam, you prove you're listening by reflecting back to Hannah what she said. Hannah, proceed."

Hannah flipped on her image and leaned toward the camera. "Sam, you think you're some big seminarian who knows the Bible inside and out. You wow the students with your knowledge of Greek and Hebrew. You mesmerize congregations when you speak, but you're so preoccupied with building up a name for yourself that you never have time for me. I'm a nobody in your world." She pressed closer. "You think it's such a great thing to invite your students over for study sessions—or your colleagues and their wives for a dessert night—but who has to organize the hospitality, clean up the house, get the kids to bed, and keep smiling all night long?"

Sam sat back in his chair. "You think I'm so focused on becoming and staying a big shot that I ignore you and the kids."

"That's the first step," I said. "What about the rest of the process?"

He examined the screen and nodded. "You feel I don't have time for you. I can see that you must feel alone in dealing with the kids, and all the demands I put on you. I do these things because I value your gifts at hospitality, and I want you to be part of my world. I want us to be a team, and I don't know how else to invite you along for what is happening."

"That's a start," I said. "This exercise is about getting into your partner's feelings, perspective, and experience. This isn't about who is right or wrong. It's about understanding and caring. It's more about relationship than being right. It's about connecting, and not controlling. It's about moving past the places where you're stuck. It's about discovering what is happening deep in the heart of the one you love."

"I get it," Sam said. "I'm willing to work on this if Hannah is."

"There's a few more tips I can send your way," I said. "You'll see how to reflect through three phrases or questions. 'What I heard you say is… , Did I get that correctly? And did I miss anything?' For the empathy part you start by saying, 'I can see how you could feel such and such, given that… ' For the appreciation part you can say specifically, 'I appreciate that you…' Does all this make sense?"

"Totally," Hannah said.

I screen-shared another handout listing the negative and positive listening filters. "You'll know you've been heard when you see your partner start sharing a positive and healthy release of their feelings—more energy, deeper breaths, more relaxation, deeper conversations, greater appreciation to you, and open hearts. Let's look at this together."

Negative listening filters.

Do you find yourself listening for the following? Whatever you listen for, you will hear.

- how someone is trying to control you
- how you can try to control others
- who is right and wrong
- how you are being criticized
- things to criticize in others
- how you messed up or didn't get it good enough
- how you can fix things (which is okay but only after you've

first offered them empathy)
- who to blame
- what to analyze
- relating everything back to yourself
- what you are going to say next
- debating or being 'devil's advocate'
- correcting for accuracy
- trying to soothe their natural and healthy expression of feelings because you are uncomfortable with their feelings

Positive listening filters. Instead, practice listening for ·

- trying to truly understand them
- their best intentions
- their feelings and needs underneath what they are saying
- what you can learn from them
- a tug toward empathy
- what you can appreciate about them
- their strengths and gifts
- what they did well
- their unique experience, even if it's different from yours
- responsibility for your own feelings, thoughts, and role in whatever occurred

"I think we need to put some effort into practicing these things," Sam said. "Hannah, what do you think? Can we do this?"

"You set the time, and I'll try my best to work with you on this," Hannah replied. "I need to start on Zoom, then maybe I can meet you for coffee somewhere. I need you to work with the kids so you understand the pressure I've been under. I've started a new job and don't want to leave that."

"I hear you," Sam said. "Make room for you in my schedule to show I care. Give you space until you feel safe enough. Let things unfold as they will. Care for the kids. Support you on the new path you're finding for yourself."

"You've got the words," Hannah said. "I need to see the action."

"You two are starting off well," I said. "Listening well is the first step to opening up your partner toward intimacy. If you know you're being heard, it helps you feel safe enough to share the more vulnerable parts of yourself."

"Got it," Sam said.

"One day at a time," Hannah said.

INTIMACY: BRAKES AND ACCELERATORS

"Growing apart doesn't change the fact that for a long time we grew side by side; our roots will always be tangled."[75] — Ally Condie

Ben and Susan worked hard to understand what had pulled them apart. They were both motivated and sat side by side on the love seat, holding hands.

"I think," Ben started, "that after the past week, we might be ready for some of the good stuff now." He squeezed Susan's hand, and she squeezed back. "I've gotten my forgiveness, and I think we've had a lot of walks and talks. The kids are happy to see me home more."

"Of course, I'm happy to see him home a little more as well," Susan said. "I know we talked about broken trust and that trust may take time to grow back, but at least we're in the same space and we've had some good heart-to-heart talks. Sometimes I just feel that Ben wants to put the gas on for our intimacy, and I've got the brakes on. Is that normal?"

I nodded, pulling out my trusty binder. "Whatever you are experiencing is normal for where you're at. There may be all kinds of influences impacting why your brakes are on more. This handout lists quite a few options that might be affecting you. See if any of these stand out." I pushed a yellow highlighter across the desk toward her. "Perhaps you can highlight a few that ring true. If it's not an issue, simply mark it that way."

Brakes to intimacy.

	Not an Issue	Somewhat of an Issue	Very Much
Too much other stuff on your mind/ /distractions/ responsibilities			
Too early in the morning			
Too late at night			
Being upset with your partner			
Low self-esteem			
Questioning your relationship			
Not feeling safe physically / or emotionally			
Worried about partner's frustration, anger, criticism			
Lack of trust			
Feeling controlled by partner			
Resentment or holding grudges from past hurts			
Keeping score			
Not enough time together			
Body image issues			
Addictions			

Grief or loss (of a person, animal, job, friendship, etc.)			
Lack of exercise			
Feeling numb (emotionally and/ or physically			
People in the other room and afraid they will hear			
Pets in the bed			
Lack of sleep			
Anxiety and / or stress			
Depression			
Not feeling intimate			
In parent mode and hard to make the switch to sexy			
Wanting more alone time			
Feeling distracted by attraction outside this relationship			
Discomfort at being unclothed			
Feeling unsupported or not accepted by your partner			
Past abuse or trauma that is triggered during sex			

Fear of becoming pregnant			
Perceiving your partner isn't interested			
Physical pain from intercourse			
Medications that impair your libido (anti-depressants, birth control pill, pain killers, or anti-seizure meds)			
Alcohol consumption (too much can lower libido)			
Surgery related to breasts or genitals			
Hormonal changes			
Desensitization by pornography use			
Feeling pressured or not taking time enough to prepare			
Fear of performance			
Feeling emotionally distant from partner			
Not feeling well (headache, stomachache, etc.)			
Fear of initiating or of being rejected			

Ben glanced across at Susan's sheet. "Looks like we might need another highlighter over there," he said, nodding his head in his wife's direction. "I didn't realize that there could be so many things getting in the way of intimacy. Do you have another sheet with the accelerators that's just as long?"

Susan looked up and covered over her sheet. "Every line has to have an answer, and that takes time to think about. I'm not sure if my hormonal changes are 'not an issue' or 'somewhat of an issue.' Or is this talking about Ben's hormonal issues? I'm assuming this is all about me."

I nodded. "Yes, this is all about you on your sheet. If you feel comfortable, we can talk about the few that you've marked as 'very much an issue.' It may shed some light on why the issue with the worship leader was so significant for you."

Susan shifted and looked toward Ben, who nodded his assent. She scanned the paper and kept looking down as she read off her list. "Let's take a few to start with," she said. "Too much stuff on my mind; being upset with your partner; low self-esteem; questioning the relationship; not feeling safe emotionally; worried about Ben's criticism; lack of trust; feeling controlled; resentment from past hurts; not enough time together; body image issues; grief—I lost my favorite aunt last month; my job; lack of exercise; feeling numb; people in the other room; lack of sleep; anxiety and stress; maybe depression... " She looked up. "That's just the first page. I think we can say I've got a lot of brakes on right now."

"Tell you what," I said. "I'll give you the other sheet on accelerators. Why don't the two of you talk through those brakes to see if you can think of any way to adjust things? I'm willing to help if you need it, but why don't you start with some good discussions."

"Am I going to be weirded out by the accelerators?" Susan asked. "I'm not into kinky stuff."

I picked up the sheet and held it out. "How does having meaningful conversations sound? How about dates outside the bedroom? How about a vacation, or watching a romantic movie? There's other stuff on this list which may not work for you, but it might give you two something to talk through so at least you know what your relationship needs and can handle right now."

Susan glanced at the sheet. "What's this stuff about the six-second kiss?"

"A German study showed that men live around ten years longer if they kiss for at least six seconds before going to work each day," I answered. "It's a health benefit that's worth investing in if you want your partner around longer."

"I like this cuddle-and-kiss before you go to sleep," she said, fluttering her eyelids at her husband. "And this section on talking about what you like might have possibilities."

Ben accepted the sheet from her. "I think the first thing we need to do is to start scheduling in some of the big rocks on our calendar so I don't get caught up in all the ministry demands every night. I need to realize that we both have the Great Commission to fulfill, but we also have a great covenant to fulfill. I think we need to find our balance again."

"If you do that, I think some of Susan's brakes might just ease up a bit. If you pay any heed to Jordan Peterson, he says his research shows a healthy couple needs to spend ninety minutes a week talking through the practicalities of their home and relationships. Plus they need at least one or two date nights."

Susan snatched Ben's sheet on brakes. "Hey, this guy hasn't said anything, but he's got a few of his own to work through. Maybe we can focus on a couple at a time and see where we end up."

I nodded as they rose to leave. "Last words are from C.S. Lewis. 'You can't go back and change the beginning, but you can start where you are and change the ending.'"[76]

"We will," Ben said. "We will."

INTIMACY AND ABUSE

"A good marriage is one which allows for change and growth in the individuals and in the way they express their love." — Pearl S. Buck

An unnamed ministry couple stepped into my office on a sunny afternoon. The man (whom I will call Burt) held the door open and motioned to his wife (whom I will call Jenny). She shuffled into the office, head hung down like a wilted rose. A women's organization I work with says that one third of ministry marriages experience some form of domestic abuse, and ninety percent of that is focused on women. Leadership is lonely, and ministry leaders can easily justify the emotional, mental, or verbal abuse against their spouses as a normal marital struggle. We never know what a couple is capable of behind closed doors.

Burt attempted to control the dialogue from the beginning. "Not sure why we're here. Some woman in our church made a slanderous accusation to my board after dropping in at our house unexpectedly, and they thought we should work this out with a neutral party."

"Burt, I can see the importance of that," I said. "Jesus was always trying to correct assumptions and beliefs. What we assume to be true is what we act on." I moved my chair in front of my desk and sat facing Jenny. "Jenny, I'm here to listen to your heart. Would you trust me with your story?"

"She doesn't say a whole lot to strangers," Burt cut in. "I can answer any questions you have. This is humiliating for a minister's wife to go through. She thought the woman was her friend. It's not easy to be betrayed."

"You're right that betrayal isn't easy," I said. "Jesus found that out when his friend betrayed him. Sometimes the hardest betrayal is at the hands of someone you think you're close to. As a minister, I'm sure you deal with a lot of marriages where a woman is betrayed by her husband."

"It goes both ways," Burt said. "Sometimes women want attention and aren't sure how else to get it. I've seen some godly men betrayed by the accusations of their women."

"Sometimes men don't understand what abuse is," I said. "Abuse is a pattern of behavior used to establish power and control over another person. Men don't always realize that psychological and emotional abuse are as damaging as physical abuse to a woman's self-esteem."

"Doc, I think you should know we don't pander much to all that psychobabble stuff."

I turned to Jenny. "Do you mind telling me about the first years of your life, and how your relationship began?"

She looked up quickly, and then focused on the carpet in front of her. I waited.

"Like I said," Burt broke in, "she doesn't say a whole lot to strangers."

"I can wait," I said.

Jenny looked up. "There's not much to say. I met Burt when he was in youth group. He charmed me. He was everything I'd dreamed of. Smart, fun, romantic, sold out to God. My folks liked him. We had three kids. Beautiful house. Been married twenty years now."

"What was it like in your birth family home?"

She kept her head down. "Normal. Dad had all the authority. Mom was submissive. There were five kids. Dad worked hard. We didn't have much, but Mom did her best. I tried to be as good as possible to avoid the strap. I knew that a good wife shouldn't complain, and mom tried hard to smile when people came around. The suffering of a woman is nothing compared to the suffering of Jesus. I needed to practice forgiveness in the same way I was given forgiveness."

"What was your church like?"

"Normal. We learned that we should have JOY, which meant that Jesus came first, others came second, and we came last. I knew that others watched me all the time to see if I was like Jesus. The preacher told me that—as did my Sunday School teacher and my daddy. I guess I was afraid all the time that I would disappoint God and go to hell."

"Do you understand what abuse looks like?" I asked.

She hung her head further and curled up her shoulders, clenching her hands together. "Can't say I've ever had to watch it."

I reached for a handout sitting on the desk. "This paper lists a few examples of it," I said.

"Is that from the Bible?" Burt asked. "Can't say I've seen any list of abuses in the Good Book."

"It's a list of what some people have gone through in marriages where there is domestic violence," I said. I gave a copy to Jenny and one to Burt. "See if you've dealt with anyone who's experienced any of these things."

- excessive possessiveness
- threats of violence

- threats of endangering children
- restricting activities
- isolation from family and friends
- forcing degrading activities
- verbal insults
- put-downs
- name-calling
- controlling money
- controlling decision- making
- threatening to harm pets
- destroying personal property

"Must be one of those secular lists," Burt said. "Our women know their place and are happy to be cared for by godly men. Sometimes women need to learn more faith and submission."

"Family violence affects all levels of society. It involves all cultural groups, ages, economic classes, and religions. Abuse can be physical, verbal, emotional, spiritual, or sexual in nature. Spouses are the usual abusers, but children see it happening. Most women never report."

Burt leaned back on the love seat. "I'm not sure why we have to talk about how badly the men out there are treating their women. I feel sorry for them, I do. It's a shame what kids have to see. The men in our world are being emasculated, and some of them can't take it anymore."

"Jenny," I said, "tell me what kinds of feelings have been part of your life."

She glanced at Burt and then down again. "I've mostly been afraid. No one would know it, though. Not at church, not at family events, not in the community. I've tried to do my part."

"And she's done great," Burt said. "I couldn't be prouder of the way she keeps our house, feeds the people I bring over, and serves in the church. Our kids are looked after and do well in school. Somehow, she manages with the money I give her."

"My faith has taught me to be patient, kind, forgiving, gracious, and selfless." She looked sideways at her husband who had put his head back on the love seat and closed his eyes.

"Do you think a wife can change even if her husband doesn't?" I asked.

"Probably not without a lot of support," she said.

I picked up another sheet and handed two copies to Jenny. She poked Burt and laid a copy in his lap. "Perhaps I should show you a picture of what is really happening, even in some church homes. This is called the Power and Control Wheel.[77] It illustrates twelve different kinds of power and explains the abuse involved in each. Let's read through this."

Burt laid the paper back on my desk. "I didn't bring my glasses, and the print is small. You go ahead and read it." He turned to his wife. "Jenny, darling, you don't need to listen to the horrible things happening out there. Keep your mind busy like you know how to do."

Forms of abuse.

Emotional
- teasing
- invalidating feelings
- using guilt
- blaming for everything
- jealousy
- threatening
- withholding affection
- waking up at odd times
- silent treatment
- stalking

Intellectual
- having to prove things
- mind games
- demanding perfection
- making partner feel stupid
- attacking ideas and opinions
- manipulation of information
- saying, "you're crazy"

Financial
- limiting access to money
- making partner account for every penny
- controlling the money
- closing bank accounts
- wasting
- creating debt
- not paying child support
- taking care of own needs at expense of family

Pets and Property
- killing or threatening pets
- punching walls and doors
- throwing things
- damaging the vehicle
- smashing and breaking things

Psychological
- intimidating gestures or actions
- threatening suicide
- threatening to kill partner
- displaying weapons
- denying he said things
- making light of abuse

Physical
- blocking exits
- driving too fast
- locking partner out of the house
- intimidating
- punching or kicking
- spitting on
- choking
- hitting
- restraining
- unwanted tickling

Sexual
- threatening to have an affair
- having an affair
- forcing sex
- manipulating sex
- sexual put-downs
- criticizing dress
- withholding sex
- comparing partner to others
- using pornography
- demanding sex as payment

Verbal
- name-calling
- swearing
- yelling
- insulting
- sarcasm

Spiritual
- putting down partner's faith
- cutting partner off from church
- using church and faith to his advantage
- using Scripture against partner

Using Children
- abusing children
- threatening to harm children
- threatening to take children away
- refusing to make support payments
- belittling partner in front of children
- using visitation as leverage

Social
- isolating partner from friends
- isolating partner from family
- monitoring phone calls
- monitoring mileage
- dictating who partner can see
- preventing partner from working

Using Culture

- using culture as an excuse for abuse
- putting down partner's culture
- forcing partner to adopt his cultural practices
- refusing to allow partner to learn local culture

Burt had both arms and legs crossed by the time I was through. "There isn't a man alive who could survive that list," he said. "Like I said, some women got together to figure out how to emasculate all the men on the planet. I think we've heard enough here."

He rose, but Jenny held out her hand. "Burt, honey, I think I know some women who have faced a few of these things. It might help us minister better if we understood how this cycle of abuse gets started and nurtured. Do you mind, dear? We still have a few minutes, and we want to make sure the church gets its money's worth."

Burt stared but sat. "You have ten minutes," he said.

I nodded. "Thank you. The cycle of abuse builds up when promises aren't kept, when excuses are made, when bad behavior is justified, and when blame is passed on. It continues to build up when red flags are ignored, and the focus of the abuser shifts to the wife's behavior. There is a rising tension, stress, and frustration. You'll find growing resentment, fear, and worry. And you will notice anger, loneliness, and hurt. Broken promises continue, needs go unmet, and then there's the next blowup."

"Wow," Jenny said. "That's like every day."

"What do you mean?" Burt asked.

"Just listen," Jenny said. "Time is passing quickly."

I slid the paper closer to her. "The blowup is when harmful behavior happens."

"And then he makes up," she said, nodding.

"Exactly. He recognizes the wrong he's done during the blow up. He feels guilt, regret, shame, and remorse. He tries to make up for his mistake; he makes more promises. He's on his best behavior for a while. He pays lots of attention to you. He is aware of his own behavior for a while."

"Hey, who are you talking about?" Burt asked.

"The people Jenny wants to help," I said.

"Then it happens all over again, right?" Jenny asked.

"Right. When you hear him say, 'I'll get help, I'll change, I'll never do it again, I didn't mean it, I didn't mean to,' then you know it won't be long."

"How would a woman know she is facing this kind of abuse?" Jenny asked.

I leaned back in my chair. "She might think she was going crazy—and feel distracted, forgetful, confused, or disillusioned with the way things are. She might feel trapped, nervous, anxious, insecure, depressed, even suicidal. She might feel afraid and embarrassed. There could be a of lack energy, and she might feel exhausted, isolated, lonely, or uncomfortable in social settings. She might question her faith and feel abandoned by God—empty or damaged."

"That's a lot," she said.

"It is, but your time is up, and I want to honor you for working with me."

"What should a woman do if she feels all that?"

"Definitely get help from someone she can trust."

Burt swung his jacket over his shoulder. "One thing's for sure. We won't send them here. You didn't help us one bit. Jenny seems no different than when we walked in here."

CONCLUSION

Sue Johnson says, "The blueprint for connection that is stamped into our nervous system by the Creator is mirrored in all our primary love relationships: those between parent and child, between life partners, and the bond between ourselves and God."[78] We have focused on the middle relationship of this triad. A love that lasts is one that is tried and refined through the fires of conflict and reconciliation.

You have seen how one quagmire can show up in so many diverse forms in a relationship. No one seasoned leadership couple fits into a specific template of collision when it comes to ministry and marriage. An experienced coach can assist in identifying both the challenges and the tools necessary to move toward a thriving relationship. The strength of a faith community, a nonprofit organization, or a mission endeavour rests so much on the health and focus of its leaders.

Relationship coach, Jayson Gaddis, says that "secure attachment is built through the conflict-repair cycle. There's no other way. Avoiding conflict actually perpetuates insecure relationships. Start learning how to navigate conflict more directly and security will be the reward."[79]

I trust that you've noted aspects of the quagmires leadership couples face in marriage and ministry. And that you have seen the hope of navigating through them until you get to a thriving relationship. The truth that the promise sustains the love, rather than that the love sustains the promise, is a good foundation for working together. The conversations I've shared are a taste of what others have faced. Your experience may be different than them all.

Through *When Ministry and Marriage Collide*, we have followed the honest conversations of seven couples.

Jim and Sharon embraced their traditional, conservative ministry in a community of faith but wrestled with Sharon's loss of her identity in the midst of life. They faced the quagmire of identity, realizing that we act out of who we think we are. Thriving involves both partners investing in their own personal growth, plus both partners focusing on their relationship growth together. They saw that clarifying who we are—before focusing on what we do and what we have—is essential.

When it came to the quagmire of attachment, Jim and Sharon focused on the need for emotional attachment in a healthy way. They saw the importance of being accessible, responsive, and engaged with each other. The emotions wheel is a useful objective tool to navigate communication around emotions so that partners can accurately understand what is happening for each other.

The quagmire of calling focused Jim and Sharon on their convictions. Understanding the source and context of our convictions is important during discussion. Working for a unity of direction for both partners is essential. Our calling, or work, cannot be elevated to the status of an idol. We need to avoid relationship poisons which can undermine our union through presenting strategies that get our own needs met. Taking personal responsibility for our use of ten soul-destroying efforts can allow clarity around calling.

Family was a challenging quagmire for Jim and Sharon when they faced the topic of infidelity. Both of them had enjoyed coffee times with others outside the relationship, but they struggled with guilt and shame when they realized how neighbor children spoke of the outside connection. They realized that emotional connections are sometimes as significant as physical dalliances. By reading the justifications people used for affairs, they were faced with their own choices and the importance of recommitting to their personal and relational growth. Dipping into outside relationships under the cover of ministry can swing into an addiction-like cycle. Jim and Sharon realized they were far more vulnerable than they realized and worked to rebuild their trust.

By the time Jim and Sharon reached the session on intimacy, much had happened in their relationship. They still wanted to focus on the health of their emotional connection. They examined the seemingly harmless emotional leaks that interfered with their love connections. This included things like any intentional exercise, games with friends, or computer time that kept them apart. Taking time to share positive, affirming, and deeply personal statements with each other, in an unhurried venue, helped restore a sense of safety and comfort. Mindset makes all the difference in receptivity.

Sam and Hannah shocked their people when Hannah walked away from her seminary husband and their children. They faced the quagmire of identity in the clash between their ministry identities at work and their personal identities at home. They felt the pressure of expectations from each other and from their communities. They realized the path of rebuilding trust was vital in restoring their relationship.

When it came to the issue of attachment, Sam and Hannah recognized the importance of bringing their full presence into painful moments with their partner instead of avoiding them. They saw that partners are looking for safe and secure relationship so that strength and confidence can bolster the marriage. The patterns from families of origin can still impact our thinking about the options for this relationship. Understanding our attachment style can help us make the changes we need. They also saw the need for healthy outside friendships to support them and to model healthy relationship for them.

The quagmire of calling pushed the limits for Sam and Hannah. They refocused their intense emotions on the issue of respect for how God had designed each of them. Recognizing the strengths God had given them allowed them to realign their understanding of how calling worked for them as a couple. When a partner feels uninvolved, unwanted, unneeded, or unincluded in the other's ministry, it can result in conflict. By recognizing and affirming their partner's strengths on a regular basis, a renewed sense of union can be established.

Family was an important session for Sam and Hannah since she had walked away from her husband and three children. Their time focused on parenting, and it didn't take long to realize the impact of their backgrounds. When asked what wishes they had, Sam wanted Hannah home. Hannah felt the marriage had lost its sense of adventure. They realized that working through their parenting styles was essential before working on anything else.

Intimacy calls us into the deepest attachment of our true selves, and Sam and Hannah realized the importance of heart listening if they were to reach this reality. Their separation meant that the path of intimacy started with the basic steps of hearing, offering empathy, expressing appreciation, relaxing into the heart, and drawing closer in a spirit of togetherness. It also meant learning to connect around our partner's feelings, perspectives, and experiences. It is about understanding and caring, about relationship rather than being right, and about connecting rather than controlling. While listening, it is good to watch for negative listening filters and select positive listening filters instead. It all takes practice.

Gerhard and Isabella were veteran missionary translators who wrestled with the challenges of a cross-cultural marriage, difficult family backgrounds, and the philosophy of a third culture impacting their identity. Accepting the labels of others left them feeling oppressed and at odds with each other. They learned the importance of loving without labels, and they learned the value that their diversities brought to the relationship. They also learned that embracing victimhood is not helpful to growth.

Regarding the quagmire of attachment, Gerhard and Isabella learned that feeling insecure and unsafe in a long-term relationship can trigger a sense of helplessness, depression, and anxiety. If things don't change, then a partner might withdraw from engagement, numb their emotions, shut down, and deny their needs. They learned that the raw spots from past relationship wounds, along with natural temperament, stress, strengths, needs, and experience, can impact us still. When we lose that place of safety with our partner, we can be overwhelmed by helplessness, shame, abandonment, and more. You can tell a raw spot has been found when there is a strong reaction to a relatively minor incident or comment.

When it came to calling, Gerhard and Isabella focused on their struggle with communication and how that affected their sense of calling. Their background, and the numerous personal issues that were unresolved, impacted their sense of call. They were encouraged to "wonder and look under" as they learned to communicate on challenging issues. By identifying their fears, wounds, or dreams, they could work to move forward. Recognizing that our calling is not to "fix" each other is important, but it is also important that our positive and encouraging comments do make a difference for our partner. Our focus is to move forward, together.

Family and culture were a natural quagmire for Gerhard and Isabella. Their cultural values surfaced in numerous contexts and created serious conflict. When they reviewed their family of origin values and expectations, they realized why they had moved to a neutral third country for the sake of their children. Issues of time, events, education, sports, and community involvement can all form a wedge in the relationship if a couple aren't committed to talking through these issues together to form their own family values. Sometimes, personalities can also play into the cultural confusion.

For the last quagmire of intimacy, Gerhard and Isabella focused on evaluating how they could stop poking holes in each other's love tanks. They came to learn that some negative conflict was not bad as long as they understood how to repair things and as long as there was a healthy dose of positive encouragement. Some cultures appear warm, and function from the heart—while others seem cold, and function from the mind. Bringing creativity into regularly scheduled date nights can elevate the intimacy in the relationship as a couple learns more about each other. Remembering high points in the past or sharing dreams about what one desires for the future will help open up opportunities for deeper connection.

Esther and Phil prided themselves on a progressive relationship where Esther worked in an executive role and Phil worked on his business from home. They wrestled with their labeled identity of 'accomplished professional' and 'porn addict,' and fought to combat shame, accountability, and transparency as they reframed their love story.

For the quagmire of attachment, Esther and Phil realized that their core fears stimulated a dance that took them into a circle of actions and reactions. By mapping out the specifics of their needs, wants, fears, hurts, and reactions, they could talk through what had previously been only experienced. By dealing with their hurts and fears, they could reclaim their sense of safety and security.

When we landed on the quagmire of calling, Esther and Phil wrestled through the issue of whether a calling to ministry in a faith community was superior to other callings. They learned about the importance of all work as a place to work out the Great Commission. A calling helps one transcend fear, discouragement, doubt, shame, guilt, and pain. It unleashes strength, courage, hope, truth, healing, and peace. The issue of calling as something other than a target helped reorient their thinking.

Working out the rules within family formed the core of a quagmire for Esther and Phil. Phil felt that Esther used rules to put him in a straightjacket. We looked at the roles of Parent, Adult, and Child used in our interactions. The issue of rules in our family of origin, in the family of God, and in our current family play out in our interactions with our spouses. A review of unwritten rules revealed a lack of trust that needed to be worked through.

Intimacy is a natural part of any healthy relationship, but sometimes fears get in the way. Esther and Phil realized this after a nightmare time away. Esther's fear of abandonment, and fear of losing herself, were at the surface. Phil's fear of being attacked choked his sense of ease. Some discussion about how those fears arose was important so they could move forward. Leaning into our partner for strength is a valuable skill when fears arise. Positive conversation is wise at this time. Facing the giants is essential to moving ahead into the promise.

Hailey and Simon, both qualified youth counselors, lived with blurred boundaries and a sense of confusion regarding what their personality types said about them as individuals and partners. They learned to appreciate the differences that each of them brought to the relationship—as individuals and as a team. Appreciating those difference is important in moving forward together.

For the quagmire of attachment, Hailey and Simon focused on the essentials of forgiveness in their relationship. When a connection between partners is stretched too far, then a feeling of insecurity and a lack of safety point toward the need for healing forgiveness. Understanding the role of boundaries, and clearly communicating those for each other, can help guard the sense of teamwork. Also, understanding what is in our control—and what's not—can help us focus on the influence we really have in a situation. Learning the art of a good apology is an important skill if you want to keep things refreshed and clear between you.

Calling was a challenging quagmire for Hailey and Simon when it came to their authorities. The two of them had to reconsider how they were allowing the influence of father figures and organizational authorities to stretch the vitality of their marriage covenant, as well as their calling. Learning how to confront others in a respectful and compassionate way is important. They learned to use the Ladder of Integrity to communicate their hearts to those who had previously intimidated them.

For Hailey and Simon, the quagmire of family centered around in-laws and their influence on the marriage relationship. Hailey's father constantly called with his advice. Jealousy, insecurity, unresolved family disputes, and subtle pressure on decision-making created a wedge between the couple. Questioning our assumptions about the motive of in-laws is a healthy practice. The importance of assuring in-laws that they are included in our life plans may take pressure off.

Intimacy can bring a challenge for any couple, and for Hailey and Simon it surfaced in the form of connection rituals that they tried to establish. They found that when there isn't regular intimacy, the awkwardness around this issue only grows. They learned that the belief systems we hold about each other impact the way that we respect and respond to our partners. Assumptions can form a deep barrier to intimacy. Choosing a growth mindset makes a difference. Frustration, anger, and unforgiveness lay a foundation for rigid beliefs about our partner, and small adjustments in our speech patterns can change this. A partner deserves affection, appreciation, and admiration. Establishing a rhythm of small, medium, and large connection rituals can assist in this transformation.

Ben and Susan, both trained seminarians who were church planting, felt the challenge of changing roles, attachment issues, and outside friendships—as children arrived and their ministry grew. Feelings of abandonment and jealousy grew as secure identity faded. Each of us has unique blind spots in our sense of identity. Ben and Susan learned why marital friendship is so crucial for seasoned couples in ministry. Affirming the good in each other as image bearers will help take the relationship deeper.

When it came to attachment, Ben and Susan focused on the repetitive cycles that continued to show up in their interactions. They learned that the comfort and confidence they felt in their relationship would allow them to reach out more easily for support. They also learned that partners can be pursuers or withdrawers, and that this affects their feelings, actions, reactions, and the stories they tell themselves. It also affects their real needs. When we become aware of our repetitive cycles and the reasons for them, we can take the steps to change our responses.

For the quagmire of calling, Ben and Susan anchored their thoughts on their theological foundation. The issues of how covenant and commission fit together stretched their thinking. The reality of individual callings for husband and wife grew out of this discussion. It is important to be aware of the ways in which God prompts us forward in life. Calling is about understanding the *why* of your existence, rather than the specifics of what you do. The story you are telling yourself impacts much of your motivation and alignment as a couple.

Finances arise as an issue in almost every family and are a fundamental source of conflict. Ben and Susan wrestled with basic concepts of stewardship and financial management since they hadn't had much to spare in their marriage. Some understanding about shared resources had to be established when only one earned money on a monthly salary. They worked to establish a budget, considered their roles as spenders and savers, contemplated the value of generosity, and managed their debt load with a future-focused financial plan.

Intimacy involves brakes and accelerators—and Ben and Susan realized they were heavily weighted toward brakes in their relationship. Having a clear list of these brakes and accelerators can help pinpoint some of the issues standing in the way of moving the relationship into healthy connections. Verbalizing these barriers, and why they are influential, can open up significant discussions for a couple. There are numerous resources available if a couple finds it hard to talk to their coach about the specifics of intimacy.

Francis and Nyota grew apart through the busyness of ministry and the diverse social causes they focused on. Their highly charged relationship left Francis anxious when they weren't in contact and left them arguing. They learned about the levels of emotional maturity in their identity, which could cause conflict, and learned to evaluate the steps needed to combat blaming each other. They also learned about taking responsibility for the way they showed up for their spouse.

When the quagmire of attachment arose for Francis and Nyota, they reviewed the Six Pillars of a Thriving Relationship and settled on the importance of commitment to anchor their sense of security. They focused on the hidden stories that arose inside during their interactions. By verbalizing their inner stories and discussing why those stories continued, they were able to speak truth to each other and to move forward.

The quagmire of calling stimulated a discussion about schedule for Francis and Nyota. Through examining the Wheel of Balance, they could see where the specific areas of their life needed additional attention. By balancing the different areas, they could see how to keep their calling effective and energized. They worked on determining what was urgent and important in their life, and they learned about the concept of putting the big rocks in your schedule before others gave you their big rocks to take up your time.

The roles within family can easily become a quagmire of their own. Francis and Nyota reviewed their traditional sense of roles and considered the value of dance steps through a regular relationship check-in. They found that a simple solution to the imbalance in their chore distribution was a game format of drawing chores that either of them could do. We come into marriage with our own collection of dreams, hopes, and desires, which soon become weighted expectations for our partner. Talking it through in some form is life-giving.

On the last quagmire of intimacy, Francis and Nyota had to confront their own busyness and the gap it created in their relationship. Numerous social causes, technology, and continuous outside calls gave them little time to invest in their own relationship. A concept like love tanks provides an easy visual to help us understand whether we're filling or emptying the emotional capacity of our spouse. Sorting out each other's love languages and making an intentional effort to communicate in a way that your spouse can embrace is also vital.

Whatever quagmires lie in your pathway, there is hope, help, and healing available if you will ask for it. Perhaps reading about the experience or conversation of one of these couples has motivated you to reach out. Perhaps my decision to choose only five conversations for each couple missed the mark for you. Perhaps you would like to see more of these tools in detail. The response from you can still be the same. Reach out to a relationship coach who can walk you through the journey you've already been on, the journey you are on now, and the journey still open to you. I encourage you to embrace the tools that are available. May God give you the grace and courage you need for what is still to come.

Maybe you feel stuck in patterns of miscommunication. Or you could be looking for a fresh start after catching your relationship in neutral. If you're feeling insecure, uncertain, insignificant, or unnoticed, coaching may be helpful. If you're stuck in past conflicts, or feeling disconnected over inexplicable behaviors, or uncertain how to understand your partner's needs, coaching may be helpful. Perhaps you are dealing with grief or resigned to the way things are—or facing transitions that leave you fearful and uncertain. Coaching may be helpful. Even if you are lost in decision-making, paralyzed by guilt, fear, and shame, or just wanting to deepen your sense of intimacy, coaching may be helpful.

1heartcoaching.com is more than willing to take you to the next level in your relationships. Check us out or refer others you know who might benefit from some time together with a coach.

APPENDIX

Personality

One of my favorite tests through the years has been the Myers-Briggs Temperament Indicators (MBTI). It focuses on sixteen distinct personality types developed by Carl Jung and fleshed out by Katharine Briggs and her daughter Isabel Myers. There are briefer adaptations such as 16personalities which can be done online. The theory suggests four dichotomies. The first is Extroverted vs. Introverted in which extroverted individuals get energized by others, while introverts recharge more on their own. In Sensory vs. Intuitive, we gather valuable information from our surroundings through our senses or through our intuition. In Thinking vs. Feelings, we make decisions based on objective, external data or on how it makes us and others feel. In Judging vs. Perceiving, we either make quick and orderly decisions and stick to them or we keep our options open to see what else might happen.

As long as we realize that these tests are pointing out general tendencies that characterize how we function in our world, it can be a source for understanding and conversation. Each type has strengths and weaknesses associated with it, and there are fun titles meant to capture the essence of that personality type. What may be confusing for some is the tendency to operate one way in ministry and another way in marriage.

If you find your type, take a look at potential ways in which you can strengthen your partnership, but also be aware of potential collision points. For example, an extrovert will want to get energized in multiple large group gatherings, while an introvert would prefer small intimate settings of close friends or even alone time to get energized.

While anyone can get along with anyone, our different cognitive functions may set us up for areas of tension we should understand. For example, it might be good to be aware that extroverted intuitives (EN) look outside themselves for ideas and possibilities, while introverted intuitives look inside themselves to discover patterns, hidden meanings, and insights. While we may begin with curiosity toward another who is strong where we are weak, there can come a time when we struggle to find common language as we try to get our ideas across. This can create friction and conflict.

Ever wondered if you have what it takes, or if you are enough? Personality tests are so popular with leaders and their organizations because they scratch at one foundational issue: who are you? When we have a label for ourselves or someone else, we think we understand how to relate and even manipulate one another. Labels take away the complexity of having to listen and connect with another human being who is a one-of-a-kind phenomenon.

I can identify as the firstborn son of missionary parents who has served in missions and produced two children who also have focused on mission work. I can identify as an author who has won awards for novels, short stories, and journalism articles. I can identify as a pastor or counselor who has served a community of faith for over two decades. I can identify as a grandfather of eleven who strives to impact a new generation with fun and encouragement. I can identify as a visionary who has helped launch nine ministries (including a hospice for children with life-limiting challenges, refugee housing, an international catering service, a childcare center, a family-centered counseling program, community outreach programs, and more). The reality is, I am all these things, and dissecting my identity into segments is like dissecting my body into disconnected segments and thinking I understand the whole.

Focusing on identity can be helpful or harmful. If one of the partners in a marriage sees the printout of their personality type as "just the way I am," it can lead to the quagmire of complacency. When I took the

Strengths Finder test, I saw that my number one strength was achiever. That meant that every morning I woke up believing that I'd accomplished nothing significant yet, but that I had to complete something that mattered before I hit my pillow at night. Even when I had three master's degrees and a PhD, had written fifteen novels, had helped start nine nonprofits/ministries, and had reached retirement, it felt like I'd done nothing yet. Did it help my ministry or marriage to put this label on myself?

Potential Conflicts in Personality Types. I test out as an INFJ (Counselor). I am most likely to conflict with an ESTJ (Supervisor). That's because we see the world in different ways. I focus on the abstract and need time to process information, while an ESTJ focuses on the literal and makes quick decisions based on now. I prefer to be tactful, while ESTJ's tend to be blunt and direct. I feel that direct communication is harsh and insensitive and tend to interpret ESTJ's as pushy and domineering. I want to look for patterns and insights, while ESTJ's focus on practical action. I may seem slow in my decision- making, and my indirect way of speaking can seem manipulative and insincere to an ESTJ. I may seem out of touch with reality and too theoretical. Our misunderstanding of each other's intentions and our natural ways of operating may seem like a personal attack to the other and can create unwinnable debates.

How do you manage this type of conflict? Focus on common positive shared experiences in your conversation. Bring a sense of respectful humor. Embrace the value in differences, and be open enough to apologize and forgive. Consider your shared values and build from there. Schedule events outside regular work hours well in advance using the concept of Big Rocks first, with the most important Big Rock being personal times like date nights, holidays, retreats.

Jim and Sharon tested out as an INTJ (Mastermind) and an ESFJ (Provider). Jim saw the world as a puzzle to be solved and constantly looked for patterns and connections. He was highly independent and focused on abstract ideas. Sharon focused on people and practical tasks. Jim seemed hard to please, and Sharon seemed to be nosey, meddling, manipulative, and emotional. Jim wanted a quieter life and put careful thought into the few words he spoke. Sharon used words to connect with her world and felt that what she said was inspirational and motivational. She spoke to establish harmony and collaboration, but Jim found it all rather overwhelming. Sharon felt Jim's communication style was too direct, rude, and insensitive. She felt he kept her at arm's length and had no patience for her to talk things through.

How do you manage this type of conflict? Schedule time to talk about your goals, motivations, and expectations for the relationship. Assign tasks based on strengths and try not to force the other to embrace your style. Patience and humor are helpful. Give space and focus on positive experiences. Reframe your partner's words and actions in a positive light.

Francis and Nyota were resistant to testing, but when they did follow through, they established themselves as an ENTJ (Commander) and an ISFJ (Defender). Francis focused on efficiency and knowledge, was direct and straightforward in communication, had little patience with indirect talk, and focused on getting a task completed. He gave high priority to his wife and children but didn't want anyone else wasting his time. Nyota wanted the simple pleasures of life and saw beauty in its rhythms, in nature, and in her few strong relationships. She liked a slower pace, loved to read, and even took up pottery. She provided excellent care for the children and used humor and tact to keep her family close. However, she often saw Francis as domineering and overly ambitious. His dreams were too far-fetched, and his drive overwhelming. To Francis, Nyota was overly sensitive and too preoccupied the smallest of details. She was caught up in the feelings of her friends and family and had no ambition.

How do Francis and Nyota move forward in their relationship? Focus on what is working between them and formulate common objectives in a positive way. Schedule time to relax but also time to discuss their goals and objectives. Give space to work out, take on a hobby, set up dinner with friends, and nurture options that stoke their individual interests. Find shared values and consider how these complement each other. Recognize their differences as learning opportunities, and explore potential raw spots and blind spots. Take time to walk and listen to each other.

Hailey and Simon tested out as INTP (Thinker) and ESFP (Performer). Hailey's troubleshooting skills made her a great at-risk youth worker. She was always searching for the reasons behind why the youth acted as they did. She loved to analyze, question, and learn sophisticated models and theories. The problem is she tried this with Simon, who preferred to live in the present moment. He brought the fun for the youth and naturally connected and stimulated the party. He was a risk taker and often jumped into situations without thinking through the facts or consequences. He found it easy to leave Hailey to her overthinking while he entertained the youth.

How do Hailey and Simon adjust things to improve their relationship? Appreciating the differences is always a good start. Simon often took Hailey's abstract ideas and made them into something practical in the immediate situation. Hailey understood the big picture of the chaos they were in and could bring clarity to what was happening underneath. Establishing boundaries, scheduling alone time to do things they enjoyed without the youth, reflective listening during date nights, and reviewing the current realities flowing around them will help get them grounded.

Ben and Susan tested out as ENFP (Champion) and ISTP (Craftsman). Ben is perceptive and creative and sees possibilities and connections everywhere. Seeing the promise of a faith community to impact his society prompted his decision to leave his promising middle management position. Susan was comfortable with the facts and was pragmatic in her support. Her technical proficiency gave her the edge in finding the tools and resources their ministry needed. She loved to solve problems and felt shut out when she was left to handle the children. Ben began to view Susan as dull, and Susan saw Ben as someone who took leaps without understanding the consequences. Susan loved the autonomy and freedom of working from home but found it frustrating trying to explain her carefully laid out paradigms to a husband whose mind kept jumping from one thing to another. Ben considered Susan to be too critical and spent more time away from home.

How can this couple strengthen their relationship as they minister? Ben is a brainstormer, and Susan is an analyzer. Each person brings a unique lens to a common situation. Focusing on the situation rather than the relationship can help with decision-making. Every husband-and-wife partnership is a team. Finding common hobbies or activities away from the ministry to build common memories is crucial, and this needs to be scheduled in ink before anything else. Talk as you walk, or create a list of issues to focus on one at a time, bringing your unique thoughts to the table. Take time to laugh and nurture intimacy. Respect the need for independence and autonomy, and cultivate healthy outside relationships. Try the six hats exercise on an issue that is especially tense, with both of you contributing to each level.

Esther and Phil tested out as ENTP (Visionary) and ISFP (Artist). Esther's vision drove her ambition in ministry, and Phil's artistic bent suited his efforts to build his business at home. Esther spun theories and ideas faster than Phil could fathom. She spun an idea, bantered and debated, and then was off to the next. Phil wanted to focus primarily on one idea that would promote his business. When Esther offered ideas for his business, Phil took it as a challenge and became defensive. Neither seemed to understand the other's perspective and things got awkward and confused.

How can this couple grow through their conflicts? Esther will need to take longer pauses to listen if she has an idea to share. Empathy is important. Phil needs to seriously consider Esther's input and stick to the facts she shares. Esther needs to give Phil a lot of space and not pry too much while he is processing his emotions. Debating is okay if you can keep it from turning into an attack. Make your communication more objective by writing down your thoughts and then exchanging lists to consider another angle. Again, take time to engage in enjoyable activities apart from the source of your tension. Practice curiosity by wondering and looking under for what might be behind what you're hearing. Ask short, honest questions to ensure you have clarity on what is being said.

Mostly likely, your relationship will involve a combination unlike the ones above. Take some time after you've done the MBTI, Kiersey-Bates, or 16personalities test to see if you might gain some understanding about your partner's tendencies. You might be surprised to learn how normal someone like your partner is.

Eleanor Roosevelt is quoted as saying that "to handle yourself, use your head; to handle others, use your heart." This is good advice for husbands and wives when things get tough.

ENDNOTES

1 Mignon McLaughlin, "Mignon McLaughlin Quotes," *BrainyQuote: https://www. brainyquote.com/quotes/mignon_mclaughlin_106607/* (November 1, 2023).

2 With acknowledgements to Bret and Christine Eartheart. Center for Thriving Relationships.

3 *https://www.leaderslifeandwork.com/blog/the-most-important-word-in-leadership/*

4 Crawford Loritts, *Leadership as an Identity: The Four Traits of Those Who Wield Lasting Influence* (Chicago: Moody Publishers, 2023), 92.

5 Ibid., 94-96.

6 Matthew 3:17

7 Bill Howatt, "Your Leadership Identity Matters," *Forbes Leadership Council Blog,* January 31, 2023.

8 Bret and Christine Eartheart, Center for Thriving Relationship coaching notes.

9 Dr. John Gottman, *The Seven Principles for Making Marriage Work* (New York: Harmony, 2018), 138.

10 Ibid., 141.

11 Dave Meurer, "Inspirational Marriage Quotes for Living Better," *Marriage Quotes*: *https://www.marriage.com/quotes229.*

12 Gottman, *The Seven Principles*, 157.

13 Julia Child, "Julia Child Quotes," *Brainy Quote: https://www.brainyquote.com/quotes/ julia_child_442469.*

14 David C. Thomas, "Cultural Intelligence: Surviving and Thriving in the Global Village," *Kindlequotes*.

15 Bret and Christine Eartheart, Center for Thriving Relationship coaching notes.

16 For a fuller consideration of the sixteen personality types and how marriage might be impacted, check out David Keirsey and Marilyn Bates's *Please Understand Me* (Hagerstown, MD: Prometheus Nemesis, 1984).

17 See Appendix for other sample types.

18 Carey Nieuwhof, "No More Email: A Productivity Experiment That's Paying Off," *Sermon Central* (blog), November 17, 2023.

19 Peter Scazzero, *The Emotionally Healthy Leader* (Grand Rapids: Zondervan, 2015), 26.

20 Loritts, *Leadership as an Identity*, 36-37, 86-87, 131-32, 171-72.

21 Adi Ignatius, *https://hbr.org/2015/05/becoming-a-leader-becoming-yourself*.

22 Gottman, *The Seven Principles*, 19.

23 *https://www.leaderslifeandwork.com/blog/the-most-important-word-in-leadership*.

24 Peter Scazzero, "Why Bottling Up Emotions Kills Spiritual Growth," *Emotionally Healthy Discipleship* podcast, November 14, 2023.

25 Peter Scazzero, *Emotionally Healthy Spirituality*, e-book, 302-304.

26 Dr. Sue Johnston, *Hold Me Tight* (New York: Little, Brown Spark, 2008), 41.

27 Ibid., 18.

28 Ibid.

29 Dr. Sue Johnson, *Created for Connection* (New York: Little, Brown Spark, 2016), 167.

30 Ibid., 29.

31 *https://www.helpguide.org/articles/relationships-communication/attachment-and-adultrelationships.htm*.

32 Peter and Gerry Scazzero, "Bottling Up Emotions" podcast.

33 Johnson, *Created for Connection*, 68-69.

34 *Training list from the Center for Non-Violent Communication through Center for Thriving Relationships. www.cnvc.org.*

35 Richard Bach, "Richard Bach Quotes," *Brainy Quote: https://www.brainyquote.com/quotes/julia_child_442469*.

36 Nelson Mandela, *Long Walk to Freedom* (New York: Little Brown & Co., 1994).

37 Dr. Henry Cloud and Dr. John Townsend, adapted from *Boundaries* (Grand Rapids: Zondervan, 1992).

38 Steve Sundby, Two Step Coaching.

39 Nicholas Sparks, "Nicholas Sparks," *Goodreads: https://www.goodreads.com/author/show/2345.Nicholas_Sparks.*

40 Johnson, *Created for Connection*, 41.

41 Ibid., 48.

42 Gary Smalley, *The DNA of Relationships* (Carol Stream, IL: Tyndale, 2007), 47-52.

43 Thriving Relationship Center Coaching Notes.

44 Brené Brown, *Daring Greatly: How the Courage to Be Vulnerable Transforms the Way We Live, Love, Parent, and Lead* (New York: Gotham, 2012), 145.

45 Genesis 2:15, 19-20; Exodus 20:9; 2 Thessalonians 3:10.

46 Matthew 28:18-20; Romans 1:6, 8:28-30; 2 Corinthians 5:17-20.

47 *https://www.cru.org/content/dam/cru/legacy/2012/02/What_is_a_Calling.pdf.*

48 Assessment tools might include MBTI (Myers-Briggs Type Indicator), Work-Life Values Checklist; the PDINH: Global Personality Inventory; Birkman; *Please Understand Me*; SIMA (System for Identifying Motivated Abilities); MAP (Motivated Abilities Pattern); *What Color is Your Parachute?*; *Live Your Calling: A Practical Guide to Finding and Fulfilling Your Mission in Life.*

49 Scazzero, *Emotionally Healthy Spirituality*, e-book, 309.

50 Ephesians 5:1-2.

51 Steven Lawson, "6 Distinguishing Marks of a Call to Gospel Ministry," *The Master's Seminary: https://tms.edu/six-distinguishing-marks-of-a-call-to-gospel-ministry.*

52 Ibid.

53 Romans 12:6-8; I Corinthians 12:7-10; Colossians 3:23.

54 A few resources that give a thoughtful overview of the place of work, calling, ministry, and faith include the following: Alan Richardson, *The Biblical Doctrine of Work* (London: SCM, 1952); R. Paul Stevens, *Doing God's Business: Meaning and Motivation for the Marketplace* (Grand Rapids: Eerdmans, 2006); Alistair Mackenzie, Wayne Kirkland, and Annette Dunham, *Soul Purpose* (Christ Church, NZ: NavPress, 2004); Timothy Keller and Katherine Alsdorf, *Every Good Endeavor: Connecting Your Work to God's Work* (Dutton: New York: Dutton, 2012); Douglas J. Schuurman, *Vocation: Discerning Our Calling in Life* (Grand Rapids: Eerdmans, 2004); Os Guinness, *The Call: Finding and*

Fulfilling the Central Purpose of Your Life (London: Word Publishing, 1998); R. Paul Stevens, *The Other Six Days: Vocation, Work, and Ministry in Biblical Perspective* (Grand Rapids: Eerdmans, 2000); Miroslav Volf, *Work in the Spirit: Toward a Theology of Work* (Eugene, OR: Wipf & Stock, 2001).

55 Center for Thriving Relationships.

56 Pearl S. Buck, "Pearl S. Buck Quotes," *Brainy Quote: https://www.brainyquote.com/quotes/pearl_s_buck_390376.*

57 Adapted from the Center for Thriving Relationships.

58 Psalm 139; Ephesians 2:10.

59 Scazzero, *The Emotionally Healthy Leader*, 188.

60 Bret and Christine Eartheart, Thriving Relationship Center coaching notes.

61 Scazzero, *The Emotionally Healthy Leader*, 226.

62 Ibid., 220.

63 Dan Woodward and Dan Reinhardt, *Let's Break the Rules: Because Healthy Relationships Matter* (2023), 45.

64 Ibid., 56.

65 Ibid., 80.

66 Thriving Relationship Center coaching notes.

67 Fawn Weaver, "The Greatest Marriages are Built on Teamwork," *Happy Wives Club*: *https://www.happywivesclub.com/the-greatest-marriages-are-built-on-teamwork.*

68 Howard Hendricks, *Teaching to Change Lives: Seven Proven Ways to Make Your Teaching Come Alive* (Colorado Springs: Multnomah, 1987), 41.

69 Thriving Relationship Center coaching notes.

70 Sam Levenson, "Sam Levenson Quotes," *Brainy Quote : https://www.brainyquote.com/quotes/sam_levenson_392729.*

71 Woodward and Reinhardt, *Let's Break the Rules*, 116.

72 Gottman, *The Seven Principles*, 128-36.

73 Sam Levenson, "Sam Levenson Quotes," *Brainy Quote : https://www.brainyquote.com/quotes/sam_levenson_392729.*

74 Available through the Center for Thriving Relationships.

75 Ally Condie, "Ally Condie," *Goodreads: https://www.goodreads.com/quotes/312939-growing-apart-doesn-t-change-the-fact-that-for-a-long.*

76 Tim Peden, "How Do We Live Out the Second Greatest Commandment?" *Changing Kingdoms* (blog), June 12, 2020, *https://www.changingkingdoms.com/post/how-do-we-live-out-the-second-greatest-commandment*; Steven Gillen, "C.S. Lewis and the Meaning of Freedom," *Institute for Faith, Work, and Economics.* September 12, 2012. *https://tifwe.org/resource/c-s-lewis-and-the-meaning-of-freedom.*

77 Jill Cory and Karen McAndles-Davis, *When Love Hurts* (New York: Berkley, 2005), 31.

78 Johnson, *Created for Connection*, 265.

79 Jayson Gaddis, quote from "The Relationship School" on Facebook, December 6, 2023.

BIBLIOGRAPHY

Brown, Brené. *Daring Greatly: How the Courage to Be Vulnerable Transforms the Way We Live, Love, Parent, and Lead.* New York: Gotham, 2012.

Cloud, Dr. Henry, and Dr. John Townsend. *Boundaries.* Grand Rapids: Zondervan, 1992.

Cory, Jill, and Karen McAndles-Davis. *When Love Hurts.* New York: Berkley, 2005.

Eartheart, Bret, and Christine Eartheart. "Thriving Relationship Center Coaching" notes.

Gottman, Dr. John. *The Seven Principles for Making Marriage Work.* New York: Harmony, 2018.

Guinness, Os. *The Call: Finding and Fulfilling the Central Purpose of Your Life.* Nashville: Word Publishing, 1998.

Hendricks, Dr. Howard. *Teaching to Change Lives: Seven Proven Ways to Make Your Teaching Come Alive.* Colorado Springs: Multnomah, 1987.

Johnson, Dr. Sue. *Created for Connection.* New York: Little, Brown Spark, 2016.

Johnson, Dr. Sue. *Hold Me Tight.* New York: Little, Brown Spark, 2008.

Keller, Timothy, and Katherine Leary Alsdorf. *Every Good Endeavor: Connecting Your Work to God's Work.* New York: Penguin Random House, 2012.

Keirsey, David, and Marilyn Bates. *Please Understand Me.* Hagerstown, MD: Prometheus Nemesis Book Company, 1984.

Loritts, Crawford. *Leadership as an Identity: The Four Traits of Those Who Wield Lasting Influence.* Chicago: Moody Publishers, 2023.

MacKenzie, Alistair, Wayne Kirland, and Annette Dunham. *Soul Purpose*. Christ Church, NZ: NavPress, 2004.

Mandela, Nelson. *Long Walk to Freedom*. New York: Little Brown & Co., 1994.

Richardson, Alan. *The Biblical Doctrine of Work*. London: SCM, 1952.

Scazzero, Peter. *Emotionally Healthy Leaders*. Grand Rapids: Zondervan, 2015.

Shurrman, Douglas. Vocation: Discerning Our Calling in Life. Grand Rapids: Eerdmans, 2004.

Smalley, Gary. *The DNA of Relationships*. Carol Stream, IL: Tyndale, 2007.

Stevens, R.Paul. Doing God's Business: Meaning and Motivation for the Marketplace. Grand Rapids: Eerdmans, 2006.

Stevens, R.Paul. The Other Six Days: Vocation, Work, and Ministry in Biblical Perspective. Grand Rapids: Eerdmans, 2000.

Sundby, S. "Two Step Coaching." Personal Coaching Notes, 2023.

Volf, Miroslav. Work in the Spirit: Toward a Theology of Work. Eugene, OR: Wipf & Stock, 2001.

Woodward, Dr. Dan, and Dr. Dan Reinhardt. *Let's Break the Rules: Because Healthy Relationships Matter*, 2023. E-book.

ABOUT THE AUTHOR

Dr. Jack Taylor is a seasoned coach, recognized for his profound impact on countless individuals seeking personal and relational growth. With a rich background as a pastor, a founder of numerous nonprofits, and an accomplished author, he brings a unique blend of wisdom and insight to his coaching practice. Dr. Taylor's journey has shown unwavering dedication to empowering others to unlock their fullest potential.

Through work with international organizations, nonprofits, and faith-based ministries, Dr. Jack Taylor has honed his ability to connect deeply with individuals and guide them through life's challenges. His compassionate approach and strong faith have been pillars of strength for those he coaches.

Dr. Taylor's extensive authorship further underscores his commitment to sharing valuable insights, making complex concepts accessible, and inspiring transformation. With a career marked by unwavering devotion to helping others, Dr. Jack Taylor continues to be a beacon of hope and empowerment for those on their journey to personal and relational growth.

If you're into reading good books, check out jackataylor.com.

If you're interested in accessing relationship coaching, see 1heart-coaching.com.

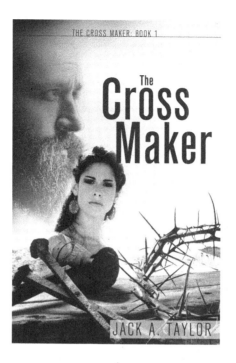

THE CROSS MAKER
978-1-4866-1856-9

First-century Palestine is a hotbed of political, cultural, and religious intrigue. Caleb ben Samson, a carpenter from Nazareth, and Sestus Aurelius, a Roman centurion, both want peace. Can this unlikely partnership accomplish what nothing else has accomplished before? Can they bring about peace through the power of the cross? And what role will Caleb's childhood friend Yeshi play in a land that longs for hope?

In *The Cross Maker*, Jack Taylor weaves a tapestry of creative history, powerful characters, and dynamic dialogue to bring to life a shadowy world. In a land where tragedy is as common as dust, triumph is about to make itself known.

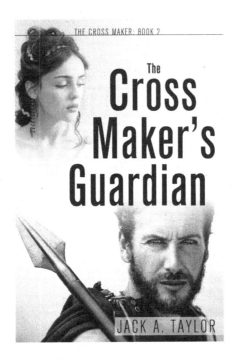

THE CROSS MAKER'S GUARDIAN
978-1-4866-1858-3

Roman legions thunder across first-century Palestine, seeking to use the power of the cross to crush the lightning strikes of the zealots led by Barabbas. Behind the scenes, a secret squad of thespian assassins are being trained—and Titius Marcus Julianus is caught up in this silent whirlwind, conscripted to be the new guardian of the cross maker, Caleb ben Samson.

Titius is fuelled by vengeance and love as he seeks to regain his stolen Roman estate and the young Jewish slave who once captured his heart. Meanwhile, voices from his past and present wrestle for control of his heart and mind.

In *The Cross Maker's Guardian*, Jack A. Taylor unveils the clash between the Roman and Jewish civilizations as they battle for life in a world suffused with international intrigue. Descriptive narrative, biblical history, and powerful characters all come alive in this thrilling read where death and love are only a blink away.

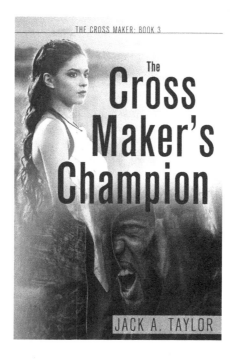

THE CROSS MAKER'S CHAMPION
978-1-4866-1860-6

Persian slaves who fight for their lives in gladiator arenas rarely rise to be anyone's champion. But the wounded Nabonidus is soon wooed by two women—a priestess at the Temple of Artemis and a humble follower of Yeshua, Daphne. Soon he must learn the truth about himself— is he a missing Persian prince or simply an unwanted orphan?

The arena claims whatever soul may venture there, and Demetrius, a silversmith, joins forces with a giant German giant gladiator, Selsus, to confront the followers of the Way.

Meanwhile, Caleb, Suzanna, Titius, and Abigail fight through their own life-threatening challenges to join the apostle John and Nabonidus in time. Soon the arena will be packed with chanting patrons. Who will still remain standing when the final blood is spilt?

Jack A. Taylor weaves his readers through a maze of Ephesian mysticism and terror as Roman and pagan powers combine to destroy the infant movement of the Way before it takes its first steps out of its birthplace.

ONE LAST WAVE
978-1-7706-9261-9

Katrina [Katie] Joy Delancey has staked her life on keeping the past and future away from her heart. But she is no master of fate or captain of her own journey. *One Last Wave* is a story about being discovered by faith and love no matter where you are, no matter where you've been, and no matter what you think may lie ahead.

NO PLACE TO RUN
978-1-7706-9786-7

N*o Place to Run* continues the adventures of Katie Delancey, begun in *One Last Wave*. It's a story of rediscovering faith, hope, and love when the maze of life seems to close in around you... about realizing that the whispers of the past can be keys to your future.

STRETCHING FOR HOME
978-1-4866-0996-3

A blissful love nest amidst a brutal Minnesota winter turns into a fiery ordeal of grief and terror as Katie is caught up in the never-ending pursuit of human traffickers who want to eliminate her from their deadly game. *Stretching for Home* is an education into the heart of missionary kids searching for healing as life tumbles in around them. Their quest for home can be as elusive as a rainbow's pot of gold. Finding old roots and spreading new wings can be a challenge.